The Handbook of Oral History

Recording Life Stories

Stephen Humphries is secretary of the Oral History Society, has organised several oral history projects and made radio and television programmes from old people's life stories. He is the author of *Hooligans or Rebels: An Oral History of Working-Class Childhood and Youth 1889–1939*, Blackwell (1981), and co-author with Gavin Weightman of *The Making of Modern London 1815–1914*, Sidgwick & Jackson (1983), a book written to accompany the London Weekend Television series of the same name.

About the Series Editor
Ed Berman MBE is the founder and Artistic Director
of Inter-Action and its 20 community arts, community
education and professional theatre companies. He is a
Harvard Graduate and Rhodes Scholar to Oxford,
where he returned in 1979 to do post-graduate research (part-time) at the University's Department of
Education on the roots of creativity in early childhood.
His many other roles include: playwright, animateur/
community artist, educational film-maker, theatre
producer and director, including the West End and
Broadway productions of Tom Stoppard's *Dirty Linen*
and *Dogg's Hamlet, Cahoots Macbeth*, Chairman of the
Save Piccadilly Campaign and Super Santa of the
Father Xmas Union.

At the beginning of the Seventies, the Council of
Europe described Ed Berman as 'the most dynamic
phenomenon on the British Community Arts (socio-
cultural development) scene'. At the end of the
Seventies, a Newsweek Magazine feature summa-
rised him as 'one of the most remarkable figures in the
world theatre . . . a unique blend of artist and activist'.

Ed Berman acquired dual citizenship (UK–USA)
when he became a British Subject in 1976. He was
awarded the MBE in 1979 for services to arts and the
community. In 1982–83 he was Special Adviser to the
Secretary of State for the Environment on Inner City
Matters with particular reference to the voluntary
sector. In 1983 he chaired the Department of the
Environment's informal working group on Urban
Parks and Open Spaces (Sports and Recreation).

The Handbook of Oral History

Recording Life Stories

Stephen Humphries

Inter-Action Inprint

Creative Community Projects Series

Series Editor: Ed Berman

© Inter-Action Trust Limited 1984

First published 1984 by
Inter-Action Inprint, 15 Wilkin Street, London NW5 3NG

British Library Cataloguing in Publication Data

Humphries, Stephen
    The oral history handbook
    1. Oral history
    I. Title
    907'.2   D16.14

    ISBN 0-904571-46-7

Cover photograph by Malcolm Keating
Cover design by Graham Betts

Typeset by Rowland Phototypesetting Ltd, and printed by
St Edmundsbury Press, both of Bury St Edmunds, Suffolk

Photographs
We would like to thank the following for permission to use photographs in this
    book:

BBC Hulton Picture Library, School Strike 1911, (page ix)
Dr Barnardo's, Ilford (page 50)
Maureen Farqulhouson, Arran High School, Lamlash, Isle of Arran (pages
    54, 71, 135)
Steven Warley, Central London Polytechnic (page 100)
Tony Othen, 107 Long Acre, London WC2 (page 126)

Contents

Acknowledgements

Many people have given me valuable advice and assistance, and have lent
me photographs for use in the book. I would like to thank the following:
Sally Mullen of Highwood School, Nailsworth; Godfrey Southgate,
Karen Weston, Karon Handford, Sonia Hill, Elaine Smith, Alison
Brooks and Maureen Miles of Whitefield Comprehensive School,
Bristol; Stephen Yeo and Alun Howkins of the University of Sussex; Ian
Bild of Bristol Broadsides; Alison Mantle of Task Force; Paul Thomp-
son of the University of Essex; Sue Bruley of Carlisle Museum; Evelyn
Hanslip of East Bowling History Workshop; Jane Mace and Barbara
Carter of Write First Time; Rodney Mace and Ruth Richardson of the
London History Workshop Centre; Joanna Bornat of Help the Aged;
Sallie Purkis of Homerton College, Cambridge; Stephen Harrison of
the Castle Museum, York; Gabby Porter of Stockport Museum; Audrey
Linkman and the staff of the Manchester Studies Unit, Manchester
Polytechnic; Eve Hostettler of the Isle of Dogs Community History
Project; Vickie Klyne of Radio Bristol; Geoffrey Langley, Chris Davis-
Ehmann and the staff of the Avon County Reference Library; Pam
Scull, Irena Czapska, Jane Dunstan, Tracy Morefield, Kathy Lye,
Linda Vickers and Anne Oakley of the Bristol People's Oral History
Project; Stephen Peet; Alan Bearne; Cath Cahn and Marcella Randall
of Inter-Action; my parents Jim and Marjorie Humphries; Anne Keat-
ing and Madge and Ken Reed. Special thanks are due to Malcolm
Keating, freelance photographer of 29 Novers Hill, Bedminster, Bristol,
who was responsible for taking many of the photographs used in the
book.

Stephen Humphries, October 1983

Introduction

This book is for anyone who wants to become involved in or organise an oral history project.

Oral history, or life history as it is sometimes called, springs from the living memory. It draws upon the memories of people whose experiences have often been neglected and excluded from history books in the past. The voice of the working class, of women, of racial minorities, of young people, even of the middle class, has rarely been heard.

Oral history can recover memories of events like school strikes which are normally hidden from history.

Most history has been written 'from above', from the perspective of the powerful, privileged few. In re-writing history 'from below', oral history can create a more accurate and authentic picture of the past. It can give back to people a sense of the historical significance of their own lives and make the practice of history more exciting and available to all.

The book is divided into four parts. Part One outlines the commitments which are central in unlocking the potential of oral history. Part Two is a step-by-step guide to how to organise an oral history project. It covers planning, recording equipment, questionnaires, interviewing, copyright, and the presentation of taped material.

Part Three is more specific. Each section shows you how to go about working on different projects with different groups. Practical information is offered on how to use oral history with school students in the classroom, with semi and non-literate people, with unemployed youth and with old people. It describes how to become involved with other oral history groups and how to write your family history using the oral history approach.

Part Four describes how to present, publish and preserve your oral history material. It has sections on how to design, print and market publications, how to use oral history in local radio, exhibitions, photography and tape slide, and how to link up with local archives. It also contains a guide to further reading, resources and oral history groups.

Although the examples in the book are primarily oral history projects in Britain, the methods described can be applied to projects in any country. More information on current international developments in oral history is contained in the Oral History Journal available from the Oral History Society (see Bibliography page 155) and in Our Common History: The Transformation of Europe, Paul Thompson with Natasha Burchardt (ed), Pluto Press (1981).

Part one:
The potential of oral history

1 Oral history – four commitments

There are four commitments which are central in unlocking the potential of oral history.

Life experience – the starting point

Each individual, whatever their age and supposed ability, has interesting and important things to say and to share with others. The first step towards realising the potential of oral history is to recognise the value of this experience. Initially this means our own experience and the experiences of those who live around us.

But the way in which our systems of education, work and communications are organised, leaves little time or space for personal reflection and the exchange of experiences. A growing number of people feel that much of what we read in newspapers, magazines and books, and much of what we watch on the television, does not truly reflect our own experience.

As Joyce Crump, a community activist in Brixton put it, 'I read a lot of magazines and follow-up serials. And some of the things they write upset me. I think to myself 'they're not speaking the truth'. Joyce finds writing difficult. But she resolved to produce an autobiography that would chart the tragedies and triumphs of her life which began in a Dr Barnado's Home in 1931. With the help of adult literacy tutor Jane Mace, her friends at Vassal Neighbourhood Centre and a tape recorder, she has written her life history, 'The Ups and Downs of Being Born'.

As in so many other locally published life histories, the main thread in her story is that of rebellion against injustice and inequality. It culminates in her leading a local campaign against the unfair eviction of a neighbour. 'I knew exactly what to throw at the bailiff. I had them all the morning before making flour bombs and we had eggs and tomatoes, and a huge banner across the

Joyce Crump (far left) with her friends at the Vassall Neighbourhood Centre, who published her autobiography.

street tied on trees saying we wouldn't allow the council to do this sort of thing.'

A voice for each, access for all

Speech is a far less restricted social skill than writing so those who find writing difficult or impossible can begin by talking onto a tape. They can then collectively edit and transcribe it. Through this approach self confidence, communication skills and social awareness can be developed.

People normally denied creative opportunities can be encouraged to record, write about and share their life experiences and their local history. Work in this field is already beginning to produce a rich crop of written and recorded material by lower stream comprehensive schoolchildren, adult literacy groups, by people's history workshops, and many others. We can now listen, for example, to the authentic voice of the truant, the tramp and the taxi driver.

Working together – the excitement of collective production

Through collective production we can begin to build a living local culture which produces knowledge by and for itself. This involves breaking through the individualistic and institutional walls that so

4

often imprison creativity and cooperation.

To do this an oral history project should try to include the following ingredients.

Democratic control. Projects should be undertaken by small groups that are given as much control as possible over the entire production. This is essential in order to sustain group involvement and identification with a project.

Diversity. A project should not be restricted to any one form. Oral history can be explored and expressed in many different ways. For instance, written or spoken autobiography, poetry, imaginative writing, photography, plays and exhibitions. And everyone should be encouraged to participate in many different activities and develop a wide range of skills such as interviewing, editing and printing.

Interaction. Oral history should not for the most part be a solitary activity. It lends itself to a cooperative approach which binds people together. This interaction between different groups talking and listening to each other can help to break down divisive social and institutional barriers. For example, a closer relationship between young and old people can be fostered by working together on books, radio programmes, and so on.

Social purpose. Although you could set up a small project just for fun, it is often a good idea to have a clear social purpose behind what is created or collected, and the use made of it. A project with most relevance will be likely to spring from the interests and issues affecting a particular group.

One recent example of this was a project on the experience of being female and black initiated by drama teacher Elyse Dodgson, at Vauxhall Manor School for girls in South London, where the majority of pupils are of West Indian origin. At the heart of the project were interviews with 23 local women, many of them mothers of pupils, who came over to Britain from the West Indies in the 1950s. Out of this testimony emerged the play 'Motherland'. It is about the terrible disappointment and discrimination they experienced when they arrived in Britain – the Motherland. Motherland played at the Oval House Theatre in July 1982 and has now been made on video. (Enquiries to ILEA Learning Resources Branch, Thackeray Rd, London SW8 3TB).

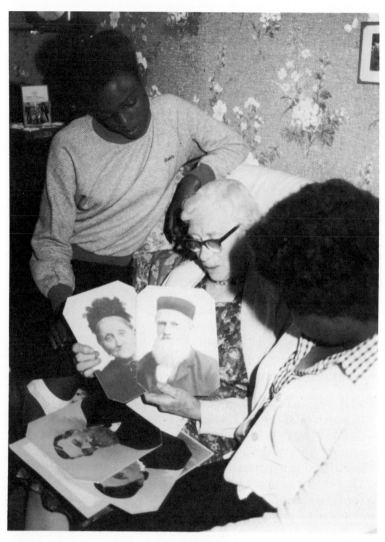

Dorothy Young shows her collection of family portraits going back to the mid Victorian era, to Alison Brooks, Sonia Hill and Maureen Miles of Whitefield Comprehensive School, Bristol.

One of the many virtues of the Motherland project was its broad vision of what an oral history project can achieve. This sort of imagination is often essential to maintain enthusiasm on a project.

A scene from the play 'Mother land'.

School students who undertake oral history projects should aim at producing learning materials to be used by others in the school. Dreary, dog-eared text books can be replaced with something that they have produced themselves to help each other. Staging plays, readings and exhibitions for other groups in the community and making video and local radio programmes are other possibilities for school projects.

It is not only children who respond to a challenge with enthusiasm and originality, we all do. So, any group working on an oral history project should be ambitious. For everyone has a valuable contribution to make to local culture in particular, those whose knowledge and skills are often written off in a patronising way such as old people, the unemployed, the semi-literate and the illiterate.

A close relationship with the local community. It is most important that the finished product should be shared with and retained by the local community to whom it is most relevant and who have participated in its making. To this end, some groups involved in recording and publishing local working class experience have created alternative centres for the production and distribution of information. Centres such as Bristol Broadsides, Queen Spark in Brighton and Centerprise in Hackney, often revolve around an alternative bookshop or newspaper. They have developed a close relationship with local people, producing life history booklets, discussion groups, radical WEA courses, resources for schools and campaigning for local causes.

New technology for everyone

During the past century the mass media has monopolised and manipulated the communication of ideas and information. But now the do-it-yourself technological revolution gives us cheap cassette recorders, cameras, video, offset litho and duplicating machines, and more recently word processors and home computers. It therefore makes decentralised and more democratic control a real possibility. We can all be writers, publishers, producers, as well as readers, listeners and viewers. New technology can be used to loosen the grip of the media professionals over what we think and give greater power to 'ordinary' people.

Worker Writer and Community Publishing groups have paved the way with their commitment to this new technology. They have used it to achieve concentrated, local sales of cheap, non profit making booklets, broadsides and newspapers. Sometimes several thousand copies of a local life history booklet have been sold in a particular neighbourhood. Radio, video and photographic workshops are beginning to play a valuable role in helping people to produce programmes and exhibitions on local issues and life history.

Part two:
How to organise an oral history project

2 Planning

The spoken word lies at the heart of oral history. This part of the book shows how to capture life experience on tape. Sections 2–11 offer a step-by-step guide to how to organise an oral history project:

Before launching an oral history project, you need to ensure that it has been well designed and that it has a clear destination towards which to travel. Otherwise it will sink. A sound structure can be built out of the commitments to life experience, open access, social purpose and the technology, described in the first part of the book.

Within this general framework there are a number of practical questions you will need to think about. The most important of these are, whom shall I initially aim to involve in the project? What particular areas of life experience would it be most interesting and relevant to explore? And, how much time, money and energy will I be able to inject into it?

The answers to these questions will determine the specific shape that your project takes. Of course, your answers will depend to a large extent upon what type of organisation you are involved in, or the groups you want to work with.

Later sections focus in detail upon the practicalities of organising oral history projects with particular groups and organisations such as literacy classes, families, young people (in and out of school), community publishing groups, old people, local radio, and so on. However, there are a number of general principles and procedures that apply to all oral history work. A grasp of them will help you to begin planning a project that is geared to the resources you have available.

3 How to write a questionnaire – five golden rules

Unless you are an expert on what you are going to talk to somebody about, it is essential to take a questionnaire to the interview with you which lists the main things you want to ask. This is how to write one.

1. Find out as much as you can on the subject you intend to ask questions about. This knowledge will help you to think of the most relevant and appropriate questions to ask on a particular subject. You should aim at writing a questionnaire that will draw interesting memories from interviewees. Before writing a final version of a questionnaire for a project, it can be useful to do 'pilot' or exploratory interviews. These can help to locate the problems and potentials of future interviews on a particular subject. If possible, try to pinpoint gaps in the written records, areas of controversy or potential controversy, and regions where oral evidence might lead towards a new view of the past and the present. If you do this, your project will be of real value in re-writing a more democratic version of history.

2. Give it a logical shape. You should arrange it so that there is a clear sequence of topics within which the questions move smoothly from one to another. For example the first section might be on family life, the next on schooling, followed by one on work experience, and so on. This flow will give your interview a more natural feel. It also makes it easier for you to guide the interview and for interviewees to focus their thoughts and memories on a particular subject. When you come to transcribe and edit the tape, it will save time and energy if information on different topics is contained in separate blocks.

Specimen questionnaire: Memories of schooling

How old were you when you first went to school?

What school(s) did you go to?

What type of school was it? (Board/private/church)

Roughly, how many children were in your class?

How did they teach you? (Prompt: did you have to do and copy down what the teacher said, or was there choice and discussion?)

Did you have any favourite subjects? If yes, why did you like them?

Can you remember doing much homework?

Was there any warm, quiet place in your house where you could do homework?

What was the most important thing which made you work at school? (Prompt: was it a desire to please the teacher, interest in the work, or fear of the punishment if you didn't do as you were told?)

Did your teachers stress that it was important to be punctual for school?

Were children ever punished if they were late for school? How?

Were you ever late for school? If yes, why? and what happened when you arrived?

Were children who were poorly dressed and untidy treated any differently by the teachers or not?

Were you proud of your school, or didn't you bother with it much?

Can you remember anything about the appearance and personality of any of your teachers?

Were they strict in the way they handled the children or was it fairly relaxed and informal in the classroom?

Did teachers punish children when they did something wrong? If yes, what punishments did they use?

Were you ever caned at school or not? If yes, can you describe any incidents when this happened?

Did you feel it was fair or unfair?

Did it hurt much or not?

Did it stop you getting into trouble again?

Can you remember children ever resisting teachers when they attempted to exert their authority?

Can you remember children in your school ever coming out on strike for any reason? If yes, obtain full details of what caused it, the aims of the strikers, the numbers involved, and the consequences of the strike.

Did you ever play truant from school? If yes, why did you do it? Where did you go? What did you do while you were truanting?

13

3. Ask specific questions. A general question like 'What did you do in your leisure time when you were young?', is often not specific enough to trigger the memory. It will frequently lead to a vague, negative response like, 'Oh, this that and t'other. It's so long ago I can't remember.' A succession of questions and answers like this can be demoralising for both interviewer and interviewee. Yet, with a little thought, one general question on a topic like leisure time could be split up into literally hundreds of specific questions. 'What games did you play in the street?' 'Can you remember any incidents when the police tried to prevent children from playing there?' 'Were there any gang fights in your neighbourhood?' 'Can you remember and describe ever going fishing, cycling, to a sports event, to the cinema, or to the music hall, when you were young?' and so on.

4. Phrase the questions correctly. There are three ways to make sure that questions are phrased properly. Write in clear, short sentences. Use words that the interviewees are likely to be familiar with. Avoid suggesting answers in the way your questions are phrased. For example, 'Did you enjoy school?', is a loaded question but, 'Did you like school or not?', is neutral.

5. Always obtain basic facts about a person's life history. You will need these in order to be able to locate and interpret their memories in a broader social and historical context. Basic personal details can throw a shaft of light on the period, the place and the people that your interviewee is talking about. The minimal information you need is as follows:

> Year and place of birth
> occupation of mother and father
> number of brothers and sisters
> school(s) attended
> occupation(s)
> date of marriage

It is best to ask for these details at the beginning of an interview. This information can then be used as the basis for a simple index system to your collection of tapes.

4 Ten ways to find interviewees

Cast your net over the whole community

1. Friends, neighbours and relatives. You may have to twist their arm to begin with, but most people will thoroughly enjoy the experience of being interviewed.

2. Local organisations and institutions. Political parties, pressure groups, trade unions, theatres, sports and supporters clubs, war veteran's societies, homes for the blind or prisons. The list of possibilities is endless. I have found such organisations very cooperative in arranging interviews and visits, and they can often prove invaluable in tracing old activists and characters who live in the neighbourhood.

3. Old people's homes and dwellings. Many of these places are full of interesting people whose knowledge and skills have often been ignored by much of the local community. The wardens are usually happy to arrange interviews and the residents are usually keen to talk about the old days. Ring up the wardens (you'll find their numbers listed under 'Old People's Dwellings' in the *Yellow Pages*), tell them about your project and ask if they could arrange some interviews with the residents. You could make good use of their knowledge of the residents by asking them to select one or two likely people for you. Or you could arrange to talk to residents at a coffee morning or an evening bingo session, then select the people you would like to interview, and fix a mutually convenient date and time for the meeting. Alternatively you could ask the wardens if they would be kind enough to distribute simple questionnaires to their residents and return the completed forms to you in a large self addressed envelope that you should give to them. A completed questionnaire gives you the advantage of a body of hard information about a person's life history, which can

save much time and energy fishing blindly for respondents, especially if you wish to interview a particular type of person or group.

4. Social and welfare services. Those who have face to face, daily contact with old people, (for example street wardens, home helps and health centre secretaries) can be particularly useful in locating interesting respondents and arranging interviews.

5. The local press. Most editors will be happy to include a letter requesting interviewees and information on a particular subject, in their newspaper. Also, they can often be persuaded to include a short feature on an oral history project. In your press releases grab the reader's attention by including as many local 'hooks' as possible – names, places and events that people will identify with and remember. The local press can be an invaluable source of local contacts.

6. Adverts in shop windows. A card in the local post office or newsagents won't reach as many people as a press release, but for a small fee, you can keep your project in the public eye for much longer. Also, if you tell proprietors about your project, they may have a word in the ear of their old, regular customers and encourage them to contact you.

7. Local radio. Local radio stations are eager to develop closer ties with the communities they serve and are willing to publicise most local projects, especially those promising to involve older listeners. If you can offer your station one or two juicy extracts from interviews you have already completed, you will probably be able to persuade a producer to include a feature on your project. With local radio stations, give a phone number for listeners to ring immediately (or later the same day) to make contact with your project. This often tends to be more productive than an address.

8. Clubs and pubs. Old People's Clubs and pubs are a rich source of interviewees. You'll find all such clubs listed in the 'Local Voluntary Societies and Organisations Index', in your local reference library. If you get to know the local pub landlords and landladies, they will probably be able to introduce you to some interesting regulars.

If you can, prise them away from their pub and interview them at home you'll get a much clearer recording. If not, you'll have to be

16

Re-unions of older people like this miner's re-union at Coalpit Heath can provide a rich source of interviewees.

content with a quiet corner in the pub, preferably as far away as possible from the juke box, the space invader machine and the dart board.

9. Doorstep, street and park interviews. Hit or miss, unplanned interviews can be a delight or a disaster. Lazy summer afternoons spent recording the memories of old men and women soaking up the sun on park benches can be delightful. Sometimes a small crowd of children and dogs will gather round to watch what is happening. Success depends to a large extent on establishing an immediate bond of trust and understanding with your potential interviewees. Failure to do this may result not only in a refusal but also a full blooded row. I have seen this happen when excited groups of young people descend upon lonely old ladies on their way to the shops. This communication breakdown can be avoided by stressing to young interviewers that it is important for them to tell the old person politely about the project they are working on, and which school, club or organisation they are from. Explain to them that it can be quite alarming for an old person to be suddenly stopped in the street by a young stranger, armed with a tape recorder.

10. The friend of a friend. Once you have set your search for interviewees in motion, it should have a snowballing effect as the word about your project passes around the neighbourhood. To ensure that this happens, emphasise to every new contact you make that you are on the look out for more people to interview. With luck, they will gather their own friends and relations into the fold. This will give impetus to a project, and will help to involve the whole community.

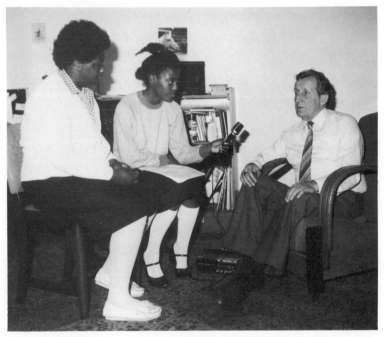

Bert Mullen recalls his schooldays in Bristol in the 1930's.

5 The art of good interviewing

The art of good interviewing is getting somebody to talk in an informal and honest way about the experiences and events that you want to explore. To do this you need to develop a rapport with them. This is particularly the case with older people because they are often suspicious of strangers and nervous about tape recorders. Anyone can learn to do this and become a good interviewer. Simply remember the following five *DO'S* and *DON'TS*. After a little practice they will become second nature to you.

The five do's

Do make an interviewee checklist. Once you begin recording interviews you need to keep an interviewee checklist (see page 20) which contains essential information about them. Keep the sheets in alphabetical or numerical order in a loose leaf folder.

Do be friendly and reassuring. Many people are a bit embarrassed at the thought of being interviewed and recorded. They will often protest that they are very ordinary people with nothing interesting to say. They may also claim to have a memory like a sieve. Don't take them literally. They are probably just nervous or being modest. Most of us, when prompted by detailed questions, have extremely accurate long term memories and can remember many incidents from our younger days in vivid detail. This is particularly true of many older people who, when their working days are over, spend much time reflecting on their life experience.

It is important to put the person that you are going to interview at their ease before you switch on the recorder. So, while you are setting up the equipment, get to know them and have a friendly chat about everyday things.

Do be clear. Phrase questions in a simple way, using short, easily

19

```
                    INTERVIEW CHECKLIST

Interview Number      ...!....

Name    .....WINNIE  PAXTON.........................

Address      23 SHIELDS AVE,  CHARD.........

Telephone Number  ....55724.......................

Dates of interviews  12 July '81, 3 Aug '81.......

Interviewer(s) ...Sally Brown (interview 1) Tom Pye (interview 2)

Future involvement ...Willing to be interviewed in
future. Will speak to Grange School if transport provided.

Times when available  Monday and Thursday afternoons

Sections of questionnaire covered  ..1—3, 5, 4.......
(in the order they were asked)

Tape used  ...Tape 1, 2 sides. Tape 2, 1½ sides

Transcription  ....Outstanding stories only..........

Copyright obtained  ....✓.........................

Documents/Photos borrowed  .School attendance
certificate and 3 photos of schooldays.

Copies taken  ..✓.................................

Documents/Photos returned Will return them on next interview

Thank you letter  ......Sent  15 July '81..........

Comments ...Slightly deaf. Doesn't like sticking
to questionnaire. Noisy dog — is happy to put in other room

Reinterview  ...10 Sept. '81.......................

Other arrangements  .............................

Summary of the contents  .........................
..................................................
..................................................
```

understood questions. Also, if you are interviewing someone who is hard of hearing make sure you speak loudly enough.

Do show an interest. This is best done by non verbal means: constant eye contact, lifting your eyebrows, nodding and smiling. If you don't, the person who is speaking to you may become unsettled and stop talking.

Do use questionnaires flexibly and imaginatively. In an oral history project a questionnaire is only a base from which you launch yourself into somebody else's world. Life experience is always unique and unpredictable, and in order to explore its contours in detail you will need to be able to respond to people's stories by thinking of follow-up questions on the spur of the moment. The sort of cue words and phrases that a good interviewer will frequently use to obtain a fuller description or explanation are 'Why?', 'Why not?', 'Who was that?', 'When was that?', 'Tell me more about that' and 'What did you feel about that?'.

The five don'ts

Don't talk too much. Be a good listener. Avoid the temptation to fire a constant battery of approving noises – 'yes, yes, yes,' 'mm, mm, mm' – in the direction of your interviewee. Otherwise your voice will be an irritating distraction to the listener and may even damage the clarity and rhythm of the voice you went to record. Show your interest and sympathy through facial expression and gesture.

Don't interrupt. If you stop a story in mid-stream because you think it is irrelevant, you may block the flow of further recollections that would have been forthcoming. Anecdotes are what oral history is all about and must be encouraged. After a digression return to the point by using a phrase like, 'Getting back to . . .' or 'Earlier on you were saying that . . .'

Don't impose your views. If you reveal your opinions, interviewees may be tempted to tell you what they think you want to hear rather than what they really think. Thus the evidence you collect may be unreliable. However, if your interviewee is a member of a minority or victimised group, then it is essential to express some sympathy with their viewpoint in order to encourage them to talk honestly about their experiences (even though you may have an opposite opinion to theirs).

Don't contradict or argue. If you disagree with the opinions somebody expresses, especially if they are on a controversial issue like youth, religion or race it is often a good idea to take a neutral stance during the interview. A heated discussion may destroy the relationship of confidence and trust that you have built up. If you lose this they will be unlikely to tell you any personal or intimate stories. If you are doubtful about the truth of a particular statement, tactfully suggest that there is another way of looking at the matter with a phrase like, 'Some people say that . . .' or 'I have read that . . .'

Don't rush away as soon as the tape recorder is turned off. This is the time to foster a closer relationship with the person you have interviewed. Graciously accept a cup of tea or whatever if it is offered. Chat informally about yourself. If you have just interviewed an old person, ask them about their family and grandchildren. Involve them further in your project if possible. Arrange a future visit. This might be the time when someone is most likely to open a drawer and hand you valuable old documents or photographs. You could arrange to borrow or copy them if they are useful for a book or exhibition.

Finally, write a short letter of thanks a few days after the interview. It shows you care about somebody as a person, and is always much appreciated.

6 Buying recorders, microphones and tapes

Cassette or reel-to-reel?

To run an oral history project you obviously need to lay your hands on some recording equipment. The first important choice you will have to make is whether to use a cassette or a reel-to-reel recorder. There are a number of advantages and disadvantages in each with regard to sound quality, editing and cost.

Sound quality

The sound reproduction given by reel to reel compared to cassette recorders has been the subject of a long and controversial debate in Hi-Fi and technical books and magazines. However, there is general agreement that a reel to reel recorder will give a much clearer and sharper sound than the vast majority of cassette recorders on the market. The sound quality on cassette recorders cannot match this high standard of reproduction, because they use thin tapes and are restricted to a single slow playing speed of 1⅛ inches per second (i.p.s.). In comparison, most reel to reel recorders have a range of playing speeds which go up to 7½ i.p.s. The technical reasons why this makes for increased sound quality are explained in a straightforward way in *Tape Recording and Community Radio*, by Peter Mount and Roger Kitchen, Inter-Action Inprint.

Although the use of a reel to reel recorder is essential if you intend broadcasting taped material on the radio, satisfactory results can be obtained on a cassette recorder for schools, exhibitions and most other purposes. Professional experts often complain of a continuous background hiss which impairs the sound quality of cassette recordings. But this can be drastically reduced if you buy a recorder fitted with a Dolby unit, and if you use a separate as opposed to a built-in microphone.

23

Editing

On a reel to reel recorder you can easily edit tapes by cutting and re-joining them. It is very difficult to do this on a cassette recorder. This is a serious disadvantage if you want to compile a tape of selected extracts from interviews which is of sufficient sound quality to be broadcast on the radio. The only straightforward way to edit on cassette is to connect up two recorders, then dub from one tape onto another. (Dubbing and editing techniques are explained in detail on page 138.) Although this method does result in a reduction of sound quality and uneven joins between different extracts, it will give you an audible sound that is adequate for most purposes.

Cost

The huge advantage in using cassette compared to reel to reel recorders, is their cheap price. Cassette recorders of reasonable quality can be bought for as little as £25 whereas new, portable reel to reel recorders will cost at least £350.

If you have a sizeable budget to spend on equipment, it is a good idea to have one reel to reel recorder with which to make high quality recordings and a number of cassette recorders to use for more general purposes.

Portable cassette recorders – what sort to buy and where to buy them

Reports on portable cassette recorders occasionally appear in consumer magazines like *Which*. Those who wish to follow the recommendations contained in these magazines will find them well indexed and available for consultation in most reference libraries. However, if you don't believe everything you read in consumer magazines and if you are operating on a tight budget, then the best policy is to buy the cheapest, recognised make of machine like a Philips, Sony or Hitachi, that you can find. The Marantz Superscope is a particularly good machine. Leading manufacturers periodically bring out new models with minor improvements and just before they hit the market retailers often sell off their stock of old models at a reduced price. The best place to buy your recorder from are discount warehouses like Comet. If

24

you want to save money it is a good idea to avoid the local high street shop because it just can't compete in the price war waged by discount warehouses and chain stores. Most cassette recorders are within the price range of £15 to £100 and if you choose wisely and buy at the right moment, you can get up to 50 per cent off the manufacturer's recommended retail price. There is also a fairly big turnover in second hand cassette recorders. If you can't afford to buy a new one, you can often pick one up in reasonable condition through the 'Articles for Sale' or 'Under A Tenner' columns in local newspapers. When buying a cassette recorder you should make certain that it has as many of the following features as possible.

Good points to look for on a portable cassette recorder

1. Separate microphone. Ensure that the machine you buy has a separate microphone or at least a socket into which one can be plugged. Most machines are now fitted with built-in microphones, primarily as sales gimmicks. Because they are placed close to the motor and to the tape heads, they pick up a constant background hum which can seriously reduce the quality of a recording. Another advantage of extension microphones is that you can hold or place them close to the interviewee's mouth. With a built-in microphone you usually have to place the recorder several feet away from the interviewee on a chair or table which makes their voice sound distant and distorted.

2. Battery/mains power. Ensure that your machine can be powered by both batteries and mains electricity. It is best to use batteries when recording an interview as they reduce the background hum you often get if the recorder is plugged into the mains. Another advantage of using batteries when interviewing is that you are freed from a dependency on electricity sockets, which can be of several different types especially in old houses. If you use batteries you won't be stymied by a socket that doesn't take your plug and are saved the time and trouble of carrying around a supply of different spare plugs. Using batteries means that the interviewee isn't paying for the power you use.

However, batteries do have drawbacks. They usually have a short life of only three to four hours and can run down during an

25

interview. So you should carry some spares. Battery power is much more expensive than using mains electricity so it is valuable to have a mains power facility on your machine, and to use it for playbacks and for interviews where the recording quality is not of prime importance.

3. Dolby unit. A built-in Dolby unit will significantly decrease tape hiss when you make recordings and play them back. However the inclusion of this facility on a cassette or radio-cassette recorder often pushes the price you have to pay up to the £100 mark. These machines are well worth the extra cost if you can afford it, but there are only a few portable models on the market at the moment fitted with Dolby units.

4. Extension speaker socket. Most small cassette recorders have poor playback facilities. But you can improve the tone and increase the volume of cassette tapes by playing them through a larger, extension speaker attached to your machine. It is often necessary to do this to achieve a clearly audible sound when playing cassette tapes to classes of schoolchildren or to audiences in clubs and at exhibitions.

5. Other plus points to look for. A revolution counter will help you find specific sections of an interview on playback and is useful for indexing. An automatic recording level control can be invaluable because it eliminates the need to adjust any controls when making a recording. Steer clear of radio-cassette recorders unless you see a cheap one fitted with a Dolby unit, because they are much more bulky and pricey than simple cassette recorders, and the radio facility will be surplus to your requirements if your main concern is to use the machine for interviewing. Look for a fairly small, compact machine made from a durable material which will be light enough to carry easily but strong enough to survive a few knocks and drops. Try to ensure that your recorder has a firm handle, strap or carrying case. This will be important when you are lugging it around to interviews.

Reel-to-reel-recorders – what sort to buy and where to buy them

Because there is little demand for portable reel to reel recorders, apart from in professional broadcasting circles, there are few on the market and they are expensive. Most people in broadcasting agree that the Uher 4000 range of recorders represent the best value for money. For twenty years Uher recorders have been standard equipment in broadcasting companies throughout the world. The reputation of these machines has been built on excellent sound quality, a lightweight yet robust body, and useful additional features such as mains-battery operation and a re-chargeable battery. The five components which make up a fully fledged Uher recorder – the basic machine, the mains-power pack, the re-chargeable battery, the microphone and the carrying case – are sold separately. If you order them from your High Street audio shop, the cost will probably be in the region of £500. But there are ways and means of buying them more cheaply than this. You can usually get about twenty per cent off this price if you buy from the discount stores that advertise in the Hi-Fi magazines (many of them are in London).

If you are short of money, just buy the basics to begin with – the machine, the battery-mains pack and the microphone. The re-chargeable battery and the carrying case are not essential, and can be bought at a later date. If this is still too much for your pocket, try and pick up a second hand machine. You occasionally see Uhers for sale in specialist audio shops, in *Exchange and Mart* and in the local press. If you just can't afford to buy one, you may be able to arrange to borrow or hire one from the audio-visual department of a local college, school or resource centre.

Microphones: which sort to get

Microphones are rarely supplied with tape recorders. You usually have to buy one separately. It is important to get a microphone which matches your machine, suits your requirements as an interviewer and enables you to make good quality recordings. To do this, there is some basic information about microphones that it is useful to know.

Different types of microphones. There are three main types of external microphone, omni-directional, bi-directional and uni-directional (or cardioid). Omni-directional microphones pick up all sounds within a certain range, bi-directional microphones pick up sounds in just two directions and uni-directional microphones pick up sounds only in the direction in which they are pointed.

The obvious advantage of bi-directional and uni-directional microphones is that they eliminate unwanted extraneous sounds. For this reason these microphones are widely used in broadcasting. However, they tend to be rather expensive.

Most microphones on the market are omni-directional and they are often fairly cheap. In fact you can pay anything from a couple of pounds to a couple of hundred pounds for a microphone. A cheap omni-directional microphone will give satisfactory results if it is correctly matched to a recorder. To ensure correct matching, it is often a good idea to ask the advice of your local dealer and experiment with different microphones plugged into your machine before settling on a purchase.

Microphone stands. Stands designed to rest on the floor, on tables or on chair arms can be bought to hold microphones. In fact some microphones are made with a built in stand. The main advantage of using stands is that they eliminate the problems involved in holding a microphone during an interview. (These problems are discussed on page 33). Their disadvantage is that they can prove to be costly and bulky to carry. If you do find holding a microphone still for long periods difficult, it is worth considering using a stand – or a clip-on microphone.

Neck and tie clip microphones. Some microphones have attachments which clip to an interviewee's clothing or hang around their neck. They can provide a more convenient and inconspicuous alternative to a stand for interviewers who dislike the idea of a hand held microphone. These small microphones can now be bought fairly cheaply for about £15, and have several advantages. They give you freedom of movement during the interview and they enable you to position the microphone close to the respondent's mouth. When clipped onto a lapel or a dress, the microphone becomes almost invisible to the interviewee.

If you place your machine out of your interviewee's sight, it can help to create a more relaxed and informal atmosphere, for he or she will not be constantly reminded that their voice is being recorded. Although it is often possible to make excellent recordings using this type of microphone there is one disadvantage. Whenever the person you are interviewing moves their arms or body, there is a risk of the microphone and lead being tapped, which will result in interference on the recording.

28

Cassette tapes

All cassette machines play tapes at the same speed of $1\frac{7}{8}$ i.p.s. But the cassettes available for these machines contain different lengths of tape. They provide either 60, 90 or 120 minutes of total recording time are marketed as C60, C90 and C120 tapes respectively. Although C120 tapes give you much more recording time for your money, because they are very thin they have a tendency to split, gum up the works inside machines and ruin recordings. The slightly thicker C90 tapes, which give you 45 minutes recording time on each side are usually the best value for money.

Also, steer clear of cheap tapes, as they frequently prove to be faulty and unreliable. Stick to recognised brands like BASF or Sony, and get them at the best possible price by buying them from discount warehouses and stores that advertise in Hi-Fi magazines and *Exchange and Mart*. (You should be able to pick up good C90 tapes for around £1 each).

Reel-to-reel tapes

These tapes are made in different lengths and thicknesses and can be bought on different sized spools. When you approach the sales staff and Hi-Fi buffs who inhabit the world of audio equipment, they often reel off all the trade jargon about 'i.p.s.', 'print through' and 'two track machines', and you end up not understanding a word they have said. To avoid getting lost in this technological jungle and to communicate with the people who work in it, you will need to know the following basic information about reel to reel tapes.

1. Tape speeds. Most reel to reel machines allow tapes to be played at three possible speeds, $1\frac{1}{8}$ inches per second (i.p.s.), $3\frac{3}{4}$ i.p.s. and $7\frac{1}{2}$ i.p.s.

By recording at the slow speed of $1\frac{1}{8}$ i.p.s. you will increase the amount of recording time you get out of the tape, but will reduce the sound quality of the voice you are taping. Also, it is extremely difficult to edit a tape by cutting if it has been recorded at a slow speed. If you want top quality sound reproduction and ease of editing, then record at $7\frac{1}{2}$ i.p.s. This is standard practice at the BBC. However, if you are operating on a limited budget, then the best policy is to record at 3¾ i.p.s. You will only find a marginal loss in sound quality, you can still edit quite easily, and most important, you will get twice as much recording time as you would on the faster speed.

2. Spool sizes. There are two main spool sizes, 5 inches and 7 inches. Most portable machines like Uhers, are designed to take 5 inch spools – anything wider will not fit.

3. Tape lengths and playing times. Tapes are sold in three main lengths on 5 inch spools – 600 feet, 900 feet and 1,200 feet. When played at 3¾ i.p.s. on a two track recorder (most machines are two track – this simply means that they allow the tape to be recorded on one side, then turned over and recorded on the other side) they give the following total recording times:

600 feet	1 hour (30 minutes each side)
900 feet	1½ hours (45 minutes each side)
1,200 feet	2 hours (1 hour each side)

The 900 feet or 1,200 feet tapes are most suitable for interviews. The one hour recording time you get on a 600 feet tape will often prove to be too short to complete an interview.

4. Where to buy them. Again, you will get the cheapest prices at discount stores and warehouses, especially those which advertise in Hi-Fi magazines. However, they tend to be much more expensive than cassette tapes. You will do well to pick up a 5 inch × 1,200 feet recognised brand of tape for less than £2.50.

7 Making a good recording – five technical tips

Having bought your equipment, make the most of it. Oral history projects sometimes use expensive reel to reel equipment but produce poor quality recordings, some of which are practically inaudible. This is totally unnecessary. Even a cheap cassette machine can, if properly used, make satisfactory recordings. The following five technical tips should help you to avoid some of the most common mistakes made by inexperienced interviewers. They will help you to get the best out of your equipment and make good recordings.

1. Be familiar with your equipment. Carefully read the instruction manual before embarking on an interview. One important thing you can practice at home if your machine has manual recording level controls, is to set them in such a way as to obtain a good quality recording. Most good machines have a dial which shows the recording level. When the recording level is set too high speech is distorted on playback. This fault is shown by the movement of the indicator into the red, danger zone on the dial. When the recording level is set too low speech is faint on playback. This fault is shown by little or no movement of the indicator on the dial. For the best results you should aim for as much movement of the indicator as possible, without it straying into the danger zone. Some machines have an automatic recording level facility. Use this if you are not confident of your ability to adjust the manual controls correctly.

2. Check you have all the equipment you need and that it is working. Always check your equipment, batteries and tapes before setting off for an interview. If you are absent-minded or disaster prone it is a good idea to load the machine with a tape before leaving. It can be infuriating if you forget to take one with you. When you are interviewing test record a snatch of conversation to find the best recording level for the particular person you are interviewing (if you follow Rule 1 you should have a good idea of this beforehand). Make sure that your machine is working properly. Remember always to position the microphone correctly before adjusting the recording level.

3. Avoid unwanted noises. It is important to remember that unwanted noises such as a ticking clock, a budgerigar, a barking dog, a crackling fire, or the roar of traffic in the street, can spoil or even drown the sound of the person's voice that you want to record. Sometimes these problems can be avoided by politely asking if it is possible to do the interview in another room or by sitting in a quieter part of the room. If you know the person you are interviewing quite well or if they seem to be particularly friendly and co-operative, you can safely ask for a noisy budgerigar, dog, or whatever, to be removed from the room. But with some people, such a request may cause offence, and you should be content with placing the microphone as far away as possible from the source of interference.

4. Position the microphone correctly. The correct position for a microphone is nine to twelve inches away from the interviewee's mouth. If it is further away than this you will lose the clarity, tone and richness of the voice you have come to record. To hold the microphone in this position, you will need to sit close to your interviewee. To do this, first make sure that they are sitting in their favourite, 'comfy' chair, then ask if you can pull up another chair, preferably a small upright one, to sit opposite or alongside them. If you do not want to hold the microphone, for example if you want to take brief notes during the interview, place it on a stand or on a cushion as close as possible to the interviewee's mouth. But, never place it on a hard, vibratory surface like a table, as this will give you a hollow, distorted sound.

5. Avoid interference. There are three main errors which inexperienced interviewers commonly make when holding the microphone, which frequently leads to interference on a recording. First, they often hold the microphone too close to the machine or have the volume control too high and their recordings are subsequently spoiled by high pitched feedback and voice

32

distortion. To avoid this always ensure that the microphone is at least three or four feet away from the recorder. Secondly, they often move their fingers around on the microphone or move the lead. These movements result in a loud and distracting tapping noise on the tape. To avoid this, keep your fingers and the lead deadly still. There are a few tips that will help you do this. If you are using an omni-directional microphone, you don't need to move it back towards your mouth every time you ask a question. Change hands with it every ten or fifteen minutes or whenever your wrist and fingers start to shake or feel stiff. To reduce the chance of knocking the lead, wrap it around your wrist several times. Finally, inexperienced interviewers often rustle the questionnaire they are using, which results in crackling noises on playback. To avoid this, rest the questionnaire on your legs away from the microphone.

The microphone should be held as close as possible to the interviewee.

8 Storing and indexing tapes

After you have completed some interviews, you should then consider the best way to store and index the tapes. The two most important considerations to take into account when doing this are the preservation of and access to the tapes.

The preservation of tapes is essential if you wish to save the voice of the past from extinction and ensure that it will be heard by future generations. The long term preservation of your recordings will be determined by two main factors; the quality of tape they are on, and the conditions under which they are stored.

The main problem involved in storing tapes is 'print through' or sound echoes damaging the recording after several years. The chances of this happening can be greatly reduced if you use fairly thick, good quality tapes. Cheap cassette tapes are not recommended for long term storage (ie 25 years plus) because they combine a high risk of 'print through' with a danger of tape deterioration or disintegration. The life span of your tapes will also be cut short if they are exposed to excessive heat, damp or dust. To avoid this, store them in their boxes in a cupboard or cabinet away from the sun and hot pipes.

If your tapes are to form part of a public collection or resource centre they are likely to be in regular use. Avoid accidental erasure, damage or theft by making duplicate copies and storing the originals. Many teacher's centres possess 'fast copier' machines which can run off several duplicates of the original tape in only a few minutes. It is usually possible to make an arrangement with a local teacher's centre to use this equipment.

However, in terms of the extra tapes you will use up, this is a luxury that most projects cannot afford. A cheaper way round this problem is to adapt a recorder so that you can listen to it but not

34

record with it and erase any of the tapes played on it. Most audio shops will do this for a small fee. Then you could develop a system which ensures that people who wish to listen to a tape sign for it, use the correct playback machine and return it. If this proves to be too inconvenient or complicated you will just have to stress the importance of preserving the tapes to the people who are using them and hope for the best.

Another essential precaution to take to prevent the loss, misplacement or erasure of tapes, is to label the box and spool immediately after the interview. If you are using a reel to reel recorder an added precaution against accidentally winding tapes onto the wrong spools is to label them on their green and red leads. The way in which you label the tapes will depend upon the indexing system that you decide to use. This brings us to the important question of access to your tapes.

To provide access to the tapes and to the people whose memories are recorded on them, you must develop a simple indexing system. A project's indexing system should operate like a telephone exchange, putting people in touch with those they wish to speak to and to the tapes they wish to listen to. Without one, there will be so many crossed lines that the project's communication and information links with the local community will break down. Those not directly involved in interviewing will not be able to find the people and tapes that are of most interest and relevance to them. And neither will you. To make the recordings and the people on them accessible you should produce two simple indexes, one containing personal information and the other containing basic biographical information. They are very easy to make.

The personal index should contain all the information given on the interviewee checklist, described earlier. If you are desperately short of time you can make the interviewee checklist and the personal index one and the same thing. However, a better idea is to wait until the initial interviews have been completed, then copy up a neat version of the interviewee checklist into a separate, loose leaf, personal index.

The first completed interview with somebody should be seen as the beginning not the end of a relationship. This should be reflected in the personal index. It ought to contain information which makes it possible to involve the respondent in future

35

interviews, discussion groups, exhibitions, visits to schools and youth clubs, and so on.

The biographical index should contain basic information about an interviewees life history. It is essential for all historians, whether they be school students or academics, to have a reference system which provides them with certain details about the person whose memories they are listening to or reading. A biographical index should enable them to trace an interviewee whose recollections are relevant to their interests, and to locate easily particular memories within the interview itself. To do this you need to distil a person's life history into a body of facts. In most cases this will include basic details about their family, education, religion and politics.

The precise nature of this index will vary to some extent according to the precise area of life experience that a project focuses upon. The simplest way to organise this index is in chronological sequence. Give each new respondent a number when they are interviewed. If you have sufficient time and money available you could use this information to form a simple subject index. This would comprise a series of lists of interviewees with particular religious and political affiliations, and so on, under different subject headings.

It is useful to note down in the biographical index which transcript pages refer to which side of tape (if you have transcripts), and to list the order in which the different sections of the questionnaire were asked. Sometimes if an interviewee wants to talk about a particular subject, it is not possible or desirable to stick rigidly to the format of the questionnaire. This can make it difficult for listeners to locate the particular subject they are interested in, especially if there are no transcripts. So, if you simply transfer this piece of information from your interviewee checklist to your biographical index, it can be a big time saver for the listener.

Another idea which helps you to find outstanding extracts, especially if no transcripts are available, is to make a note of any stories that you feel are of special interest. The biographical index can be easily put together using a loose leaf folder or a box of cards. An example of what one sheet might look like is given on the opposite page.

If you wish to develop a more comprehensive index to your

36

BIOGRAPHICAL INDEX

Interview Number .....1.....

Year of Birth ....1899...... Place of Birth Yeovil, Somerset

Father's occupation ...Agricultural labourer......

Mother's occupation Domestic servant before marriage

Brothers ......2.........Sisters 5 (2 died in childhood)

Education ...Yeovil Board School until age 14...

Occupations (with dates) Domestic servant 1913-1925
...Part time Shop Assistant 1925 →............

Politics ...Labour Party member...........

Religion ...Methodist...................

Year of marriage .....1925..... Children 3 boys, 1 girl.

Husband/wife's occupation(s) Thatcher up to 1952

Stories of special interest School strike, running
away from home, rough music in village.....

Order of questionnaire 1-3, 5, 4, 6-8.......

Tapes	Sides	Transcript pages	Notes
1	1	1-12	spoiled by
	2	12-25	dog barking
2	1	25-40	
	2	41-54	
3	1	55-67	
	2	68-80	slight
			interference on tape

collection, of the type used in major public archives, the books listed on page 155 will advise you how to do this. But the system described here should prove quite adequate for most purposes. However, if there is a library, museum, record office or history group in your area with a collection of tapes, you should consider collaborating with them. They may have resources that could be channelled into your project, and which might extend its influence and result in the formation of a major local archive.

One final word of warning. The information you hold about a person's life history could conceivably be mis-used. For example the police or the press may use it to incriminate or harrass them. Some left wing political activists I have interviewed have quite rightly been concerned about this, and it is your responsibility to protect them against any harassment or victimisation, by being careful about who you disclose information to.

More commonly people sometimes wish to remain anonymous or retain their privacy because in their interviews they might make critical comments about family members, neighbours or former employers who are still alive, and they do not want these damaging quotations attached to them. For these reasons each entry in an index which is publicly available should be numbered but not named. Discretion should be used when disclosing its contents. This brings us to the important question of copyright.

9 Copyright – formal and informal agreements

The law of copyright governs who has the right of access to and use of material. Copyright law is a very complex and controversial area. But for the purposes of history projects there are two broad ways of approaching it. You can either make a formal or an informal agreement with the person whose life history you have collected. Each has certain advantages and disadvantages.

1. A formal agreement states the rights and responsibilities of both parties (ie interviewee and project organisers) with regard to the material. The signature of both the interviewee and one of the

```
                    COPYRIGHT AGREEMENT

I hereby give to the Chard People's History Group the right
to use my taped recollections/copies of my photos and docu-
ments, for the following purposes:- publication, broadcast-
ing, and use in schools, exhibitions and talks.  I am also
willing for researchers and members of the public interest-
ed in the material to be given access to it.  It is most
likely that the material will be used solely by local peop-
le and organisations, but should any commmercial publisher
or broadcasting company wish to make use of it, a standard
fee for me or my next of kin will be negotiated.

While accepting the above arrangement, I wish the following
restrictions to be placed on the use of the material:-

Pages 10-12 of the transcript and the corresponding
tape shall not be broadcast or published in any form.

I do/do not wish my name to be used in connection with the
material (delete as applicable)   Steve Smith
Signed  Jennie Paxton  ....................... Chard
        ..................... People's History Group
```

organisers are placed on the agreement, in recognition of a binding commitment to it. It should specify the use that is to be made of the material and any restrictions that the interviewee wishes to be placed on it. It should also give the interviewee the opportunity to remain anonymous if they so wish, and should promise to secure basic rights for them in the event of the material being extensively used by commercial publishing or broadcasting companies. An example of what such an agreement might look like is given on the previous page.

The advantage of a formal agreement is that it speeds up and smooths out the whole process of organising access to the material, because everyone knows in advance for what purposes and under what conditions it can be used. Also, it can avoid unforseen legal wrangles in the future. For example it is sometimes difficult to obtain permission from relatives to use the material.

2. An informal agreement involves no binding documents, but is based instead on a verbal understanding between informant and interviewer. It should embrace the same sort of rights and responsibilities contained in the formal agreement described above, but in this case the arrangement is taken on trust. The interviewer makes a note of any restrictions that the interviewee wishes to be placed on the use of the material and files it away in the personal index. Should there be a request to use the material in a different manner from that originally understood by the interviewee permission must be sought once again. Most British oral history projects have, to date, used this informal approach. It is slower and in the long term involves more work (exchanges of letters and phone calls) than the formal agreement. Its great advantage is that it dispenses with legal documents that often arouse suspicion and fear in many people's minds. I know of one woman who tore up a formal agreement in disgust, feeling that to sign it would be to taint the personal relationship she had developed with the man who had recorded her life story.

10 The question of transcription

It is very important to transcribe your tapes, either in whole or in part, in order to provide easy access to the ideas and information they contain. Before embarking on any transcribing there are important questions to consider, such as:

what equipment should I use?
what type of transcript do I want to produce?
who should do the transcribing?
how do I best capture the spoken word in a written form?

What equipment to use?

To play back the tapes for transcription you can use the reel to reel or cassette machine on which you made the original recording. If you are transcribing in a room where a low level of noise is required or where there are other people using tape recorders, you can avoid problems by buying a cheap pair of headphones or an earpiece to fit into the appropriate socket on your machine. A few of the more expensive recorders have an attachment whereby you can fit a stop/start/and reverse foot pedal for playback. This is a big time saver, especially if you are typing the transcripts, as it leaves both hands free and enables you to move back easily and quickly to phrases that are difficult to understand on first hearing. One of the most reputable cassette recorders on the market which has this facility is the National Panasonic RV-2600S dictating machine.

As well as thinking about suitable playback equipment, you must also decide whether the transcripts are to be hand or typewritten. The latter has several advantages. It makes possible a clearer and more attractive finished product, suitable for a public archive. By using carbon paper you can easily reproduce three copies of the transcript – a top copy to be kept as part of the collection, a second to be given to the interviewee, and a third to be cut up to form a subject index. Typewriters are commonplace and relatively cheap items of equipment. Many individuals or organisations have access to them, or if needs be you can buy a reasonable second hand machine for under £50.

However, there are some disadvantages. If you don't possess foot controls, it is far quicker to produce a handwritten transcript. You use one hand to operate the machine and transcribe the tape with the other hand. Some people, may find using a typewriter difficult and unnecessary. For them, handwriting may be a more useful and beneficial way of approaching transcription. And there are some situations, particularly in which a group of people wish to transcribe different tapes simultaneously, for example in a school classroom, where it will often not be possible or desirable for transcripts to be typewritten. In sum, the decision whether to produce typewritten or handwritten notes should be governed by the purpose and particular circumstances of your project. In many projects there will probably be a place for both.

Transcribing an interview.

What type of transcript to produce?

There are two main types of transcripts – complete or edited. A complete transcript includes everything that is said by the interviewer and interviewee on the tape. All things being equal, this is clearly the most valuable form of transcript. When producing an edited transcript it is impossible to take account of the interests of everyone. An extract a transcriber omits as irrelevant might have been of interest and importance to a future reader. However, transcribing is a very time consuming and complex task. It can take between five and twelve hours to transcribe each hour of recorded tape. When typed up, using double spacing, one hour of tape usually makes between fifteen and thirty pages of transcript on A4 paper, the length varying according to the rhythm of the interviewee's speech. Even if you are selective about which interviews to transcribe, full transcripts can be a great drain on the resources of your project.

Most projects, particularly if they are undertaken as voluntary activities, cannot afford to invest this amount of time and energy in transcription, and have to be content with some form of edited transcript for most recordings. The best way to make an edited transcript is to summarise the life history of the interviewee and introduce direct quotation only when you feel an anecdote or opinion is particularly interesting or relevant to the purpose of your project. The detail with which you choose to summarise the interviewees responses and the frequency with which you use quotation will depend upon the time you have available. An edited transcript might be anything from a couple to several dozen pages in length.

Who should do the transcribing?

The translation of speech into sentences and pauses into punctuation is an art that demands concentration and skill. It is best undertaken by someone with a direct interest and involvement in the content of the tape – preferably the person who actually did the interview. They should be able to understand the difficult sentences which because of a speedy rhythm of speech, a strong dialect or a poor recording, are inaudible to anyone else's ear. They will also know which parts of the tape contain particularly vivid recollections that deserve to be transcribed in full. Where

43

the life history of a person is being recorded in order to help develop their reading and writing skills, they should clearly play an important role in the transcription and editing of the tape. This is described in more detail on page 83.

How to capture the spoken word in a written form

There are two different approaches to how best to do this. You can produce either an 'authentic' or a 'corrected' transcript. An authentic transcript often has slightly more weight as a piece of historical evidence. But neither of them can be said to be categorically 'right' or 'wrong'. For in choosing which type of transcript to produce, you not only have to take account of the historian's demand for precise accuracy of detail but consider the needs of the transcriber and reader as well. The reader will usually require a more flexible approach and therefore, corrected transcripts are more straightforward. As long as certain basic rules of transcription are observed, these also constitute an acceptable form of historical evidence. Most projects, particularly if they are not organised exclusively by and for professional historians, will probably use both types of transcription at one time or another.

Authentic transcripts aim to record faithfully the content and intonation of an interviewee's speech. The spoken word does not have the same logical drive as the written word. In speech there is far more digression, repetition and personalisation than in written prose. This approach to transcription stresses the importance of recording people's words in the order in which they are spoken, even though this may involve transcribing long unfinished sentences, gramatically incorrect phrases and constant repetitions like 'you know' and 'I said'. No attempt is made to force the speech into a grammatical straightjacket, and the punctuation is determined by the flow of a story, not the conventions of written prose.

When using this method it is standard practice to indicate any cuts you have made by inserting a short dotted line. Occasional phonetic spelling is used to convey the sound of a local dialect and the voice of an interviewee. The advantage of this approach is that it captures the rhythms of speech, so that when you look at a transcript it reads as if somebody is talking to you. An example of this type of transcription follows which is an extract from an interview I did with a retired bus conductress, Ada Iles. She is talking about courting and sex in her young days in Bristol during the early part of the century.

> My father used to say to me, 'its like a lot of tom cats', because we had a back alley, and he did say 'go out there and there's boys waiting for she, go out the front they'm other side.' I'd say, 'see thee on top of the lane, see thee in the back alley, see thee down by the shops', all on the same night. And I'd pick out the one I did think, oh he d'look the smartest of the lot, I'd a pass the others and go out with that 'un . . . But you'd never see a girl kissing a fella goodnight or having a bit of necking in those days. They used to get in dark alleys, it was all under cover but the self same things did happen.

Interviewer. So people did have sex before marriage in those days?

> Yes. Only if they was caught and the girl got into trouble, nine times out of ten she was either, her parents did chuck her out on the road, or she was sent away to a home. But nature was the same as it is today, only same as I said, everything was under cover. Today its out in the open, which is a damn good thing in my ideal, because they know what they're about, and they know the risks they're taking. Well, we was so ignorant in those days, that they knew they was doing what they shouldn't ought to be doing, but they didn't realise the seriousness of it, they was so ignorant.

The narrative form, the grammatical irregularities and the dialect words in this extract, demand a higher level of concentration and adaption by the reader than in a passage of standard English. But the extra effort required is well worthwhile because we can sense the humour and the warmth of this lady so directly, it is almost as if we are sitting next to her. This type of transcription is eminently suitable for quotation by oral historians in their books and articles, and a number of major collections have, quite rightly, been transcribed along these lines. However, there are some circumstances in which attempts to make authentic transcripts can prove to be troublesome and counter-productive. This is where a corrected form of transcript may be more beneficial.

Corrected transcripts aim to record the content of an interview, as far as possible, in the words of the interviewee. In order to make an extract clear, continuous and comprehensible, they may use some connecting words that were not on the original recording.

This is justifiable as long as the insertions are minor ones, and to the extent that the overall content and character of the original speech is preserved. It is indefensible if there is a change of meaning or if the memories are not recognisably those of the respondent.

Let us take one common example of the need for a corrected transcript. You wish to shape an autobiography out of a series of interviews with somebody. When playing the tape back you find many question and answer sequences like the following:

> *Question.* 'Can you ever remember going on strike when you were at school?'
> *Answer.* 'Yes, I remember we did once, I think it was in the autumn of 1911, the year the dockers came out.' (There follows a moving account of a mass pupil protest against the infliction of corporal punishment in schools – but which does not make use of the term school strike).

In this instance it would be quite proper to begin this story, 'I remember we did have a school strike once, it was in the autumn of 1911 . . .' If you are trying to construct an autobiography from oral testimony, there are many occasions when this type of minor adjustment is necessary in order to maintain the clarity and flow of the narrative. To ensure that no errors of fact or interpretation are made, the corrected transcript should be shown to the person whose life history you are writing, to obtain his or her approval.

Let us consider another reason for corrected transcripts. Many schoolchildren find authentic transcripts with their phonetic spelling, grammatical irregularities and dotted lines, difficult or almost impossible to understand on first reading. This can act as a powerful disincentive to all but the most able and confident readers. Let us also include here adults who rarely read books, and might be tempted to buy the life history of a local contemporary of theirs. They may be dissuaded when they leaf through the pages and find unfamiliar and confusing sentences. If oral history is to reach these people, young and old alike, and if it is to attract their attention and interest, it must be written in a fairly clear and straightforward way. It is foolish to slavishly transcribe every digression, repetition and grammatical error if your aim is to excite the imagination of those who are uninitiated into the complexities of narrative forms of speech. Surely, here is a strong case for the corrected transcript.

11 Evaluation, presentation and interpretation, the final stage

Once you have begun to collect, catalogue and transcribe your taped material, you are in a position to shape it into whatever form of life history best serves your purpose. In many ways the evaluation, presentation and interpretation of the material you have collected is the most exciting yet demanding part of the project. Let us look at each part of this final process in turn.

Evaluation

The first question you must consider is, how reliable is your material? All forms of historical evidence, whether they be press reports, social investigations, diaries, contemporary letters, autobiography or oral testimony, are subject to bias and distortion of a conscious or unconscious nature. There are three general rules that historians follow to check the reliability of their source material. You should, as far as possible, also adopt them.

1. Look for internal consistency. Check that there are no major contradictions or inconsistencies of detail within the interview as a whole. Some people occasionally produce stereotyped generalisations that must be seen as symbolic evidence of attitudes, but inaccurate in terms of factual detail. An older person's long term memory is usually most reliable in recalling details of their everyday routine in the family, at school and at work. They can often recount incidents and experiences that profoundly influenced the development of their character or the shape of their life. But they are usually far less reliable in matters of precise chronology and in placing events that did not directly affect them.

2. Cross check with other sources. A series of interviews undertaken in a particular locality will provide numerous opportunities to cross check factual details. Also, documentary sources can sometimes be tapped to provide support for a statement by an interviewee. For example if somebody recalls being involved in a school strike you can often obtain confirmation by looking in the school's log or punishment book, or the local press. On a more general level, we can make an informed guess about the likely truth of someone's memories by placing them in the wider context of what we already know about the social conditions of a particular historical period. However, if there is a discrepancy between written and oral evidence it does not necessarily mean that the latter is incorrect or unreliable. Indeed the real value of oral history is its power to lead us towards a truer understanding of the past and to throw a shaft of light on the distortions and gaps in the official records and in conventional histories.

3. Be aware of potential bias.
Distortions can appear in many different areas and can operate on many different levels. For example, some people may try to reinforce a respectable self image by painting a rosy picture of their past.

Former public figures will sometimes try to create a favourable impression of their actions and achievements, which may lead them to falsify or suppress incidents which would reflect badly on them. Older people's memories of childhood and youth will be influenced by their adult perspective and by the values they have subsequently absorbed. This can sometimes distort their assessments of the past. For although they often celebrate the discipline and respect for authority of the 'good old days', they also often have recollections of acts of rebellion and revenge against repressive adults when they were young, which contradicts this stereotype of respect for authority.

Another potential source of bias lies in the danger of selecting people who are unrepresentative of the group, locality or industry that you are investigating. To avoid this try to obtain a broad cross section. For example, the correct proportion of men and women, so that your sample reflects the original composition of a social group. Some research projects may wish to achieve even greater accuracy by taking a 'quota sample'. (For an explanation how to do this see the books listed on page 155).

However, despite these difficulties, you can usually test the validity of people's memories to a far greater extent than you can with documentary sources. Questions which must be asked to assess the authenticity of a piece of documentary evidence – Is it a forgery? Who was the author? For what social purpose was it produced? What are the likely areas of distortion? – can be more confidently answered for oral evidence. This is because the interview situation offers the advantage of a dialogue between the historian and his/her source of evidence, in which cross-questioning and requests for more detail are possible. In comparison documentary evidence is a controlled, one way form of communication.

Presentation

Whether your aim is to produce a book, illustrate a talk, stage an exhibition or compile a series of radio programmes (or all of these), you have to decide what is the most suitable and effective way of presenting your material.

There are three basic forms of presentation to choose from. Most projects will use a combination of these, and will adopt different approaches in different circumstances.

1. The single life history. This form gives full expression to someone with an exceptionally fertile memory and particularly interesting life experiences. One example of this approach is Raphael Samuel's *East End Underworld: Chapters in the Life of Arthur Harding*, Routledge and Kegan Paul (1981). Drawn from transcripts of tape recorded reminiscences taken over a six year period, it documents the progress from pickpocket to prisoner of a man brought up in the Jago, the most infamous criminal slum of late-Victorian London.

It was early in February 1902. The time was about 8.30 p.m., the street was dark, being badly lit by gas lamps. A large horse-drawn cart was slowly passing along in the roadway, loaded with large bales of rags which were bulging out at the sides. Nobody could mistake the large bales for anything but what they were – rags. I noticed a man walking behind the cart, and attempting to pull one of the bales off. It was One-eyed Charlie, the leader of a well-known gang of thieves who frequented Clark's coffee shop. He seemed to be having some difficulties in clearing the sack from the ropes, but eventually got it down on the road. Charlie recognised me as one of the young boys belonging to Brick Lane and asked me

49

Arthur Harding as a Barnardo boy in 1896, aged 9.

to give him a hand with the sack. I did so willingly. Suddenly, from nowhere, a policeman appeared and blew his whistle. He seized Charlie by the arm and they began struggling. Eventually he was taken to Commercial Street police station and charged with stealing a bale of rags, valued at 18s. I ran off, but unfortunately the policeman who had arrested Charlie recognised me and the next day I was arrested. I was taken to Commercial Street police station and put in a cell for the night. No food was given me and no one was sent to tell my mother where I was.

The next morning I was taken by Black Maria to Worship Street magistrate's court. When the time came for me to appear the jailor led me to a large dock where I stood to attention. The clerk of the court read out the charge and asked me to plead 'guilty' or 'not guilty'. I pleaded 'not guilty'. PC Stevens then had a conversation with the magistrate which was quite unintelligible to me. The magistrate then remanded me to appear the next week with Charles Walker. No bail. The trial eventually took place on the 4 March 1902 at the North London Sessions, Clerkenwell. There were two judges at that court. In No. 1 a Mr O'Connell was the chairman. He had the reputation of being a humane judge. No. 2 court was presided over by a lawyer named Mr Loveland Loveland, a man devoid of sympathetic impulses. In Holloway, where I had been held on remand, the old timers advised me to plead guilty because then I would come up before Mr O'Connell, who had a good reputation among old offenders. Unfortunately I did not take their advice but pleaded 'not guilty' and came up before Mr Loveland Loveland. The case lasted about an hour. I was so scared that I could not speak the words 'not guilty' when called. Walker received three years penal servitude, and I, being a first offender, was given twelve months hard labour.

I was sent to Wormwood Scrubs and placed in an empty cell. The first thing I noticed was that I had no bed to sleep on. Some eminent Christian with the love of Christ in his heart had ordained that we were to sleep on a plank of wood. He had also made hard work our daily fare. In the first month we were employed every day picking oakum. It was a painful task which made the fingers sore, and sitting on a wooden stool for hours on end can be very painful. The next month we were sewing coalbags. After that the work was easier – mailbags. We were unlocked for an hour's exercise each day, but the only other time we were let out was to go to chapel. This happened once a day and twice on Sunday. The congregation numbered 500 or more and the warders sat on a raised platform facing them. The congregation joined in the service with great enthusiasm and I was amazed at the fervour. The whole atmosphere was like the 'Edinburgh Castle' meetings I had been to in Limehouse, when I was a Barnardo boy. I could not join in – I was filled with bitterness against the warders and the prison governor and all those who had locked me up. I got ill from the stuffy atmosphere of the cell and with the help of a young prison doctor I was able to have a little more time in the prison grounds, getting a job carrying coal to different furnaces.

On 18 January 1903 I was released. I was given a gratuity of ten shillings – a gold half sovereign – and given back my clothes. At the gate there was a lady who gave me a tract and a ticket for a free breakfast. 'God bless you,' she said (the text, in red letters, was 'I say unto Ye, that he that is without sin, let him cast the first stone').

2. The collection of life histories or stories. This form is particularly suitable for presenting more commonplace experiences, which are not so remarkable or rich in detail as in single autobiographical accounts. The stories are edited and then combined to focus upon a particular period, place, group or theme. Some examples of books using this approach are Thea Thompson, *Edwardian Childhoods*, Routledge and Kegan Paul (1980); Mary Chamberlain, *Fenwomen*, Routledge and Kegan Paul (1983); and Studs Terkel, *Working*, Wildwood House (New York 1974). Melvyn Bragg, *Speak for England*, Secker and Warburg (1976) and Sheila Rowbotham and Jean McCrindle, *Dutiful Daughters*, Allen Lane (1978).

3. The analysis of life stories. This form interweaves quotation with analysis, and uses life story extracts to construct arguments and to try to develop fresh historical interpretations. It creates a multi-dimensional picture of the past by drawing on oral and documentary evidence from many different sources. Examples of books using this approach are Paul Thompson, *The Edwardians*, Weidenfeld and Nicolson (1975); Jerry White, *Rothschild Buildings*, Routledge and Kegan Paul (1980), and my own *Hooligans or Rebels? An Oral History of Working Class Childhood and Youth, 1889–1939*, Blackwell (1981).

Interpretation

Because oral history can dig deep into areas of life experience that remain hidden from documentary methods, it can extract nuggets of historical truth from the quarries of the past. The insights it can give into problems such as class, sexual and racial inequality can teach us important lessons, and help us to exercise greater control over our futures. However, this power is only unleashed if at some stage in the process of recording and writing life histories, there is some attempt to explain why it all happened in the way it did.

52

A new interpretation of the past will not suddenly 'emerge' from a series of interviews. We as authors or as members of a collective, must search for it through argument and analysis – preferably in collaboration with the people whose life histories we are interpreting.

This explanatory thrust is clearly most important in the third form of presentation described above, the cross analysis of life stories. But it should be present in all oral history projects. In this way the history we create can avoid the dead ends of aimless fact collecting and grand theorising, that trap so many historians and sociologists. We can then start to build new explanations of the past out of the raw material of people's life experience.

Here is an example of the analysis of people's memories of rebellion at school taken from my own book, *Hooligans or Rebels?* (p. 72).

Perhaps the most moving and most unusual tradition of resistance that developed in response to the widespread use of corporal punishment in state schools was the emergence of an elaborate children's folklore, which celebrated the magical power of various substances such as salt or orange peel either to snap the cane or to immunize the victim from any sensation of pain if they were applied to the skin in the correct ritualistic manner. Although most children's beliefs – for example, faith in the power of a hair, when placed across the palm of the hand, to snap a bamboo cane – were clearly mythical, it is possible that other practices, such as the regular rubbing of resin into the hands, did in fact toughen the skin to such an extent that it occasionally broke the cane on impact. Like a number of other old people, Bristolian Winnie Ettle, recalled:

'Sometimes when I knew I was going to get the cane – we always 'ad a bit of resin – we be rubbing this resin on our hands. "Hold your hand out." They'd give you the cane, but it would snap the cane an' you never felt it.'

But as children grew older, they gradually became aware of the unreliable and imaginary nature of much of this resistance and resorted to more practical strategies, such as hiding or stealing the teacher's cane. However, they often discovered such devious tactics to be equally ineffective, as Reg Summerhayes, recalling his Bath school days in the early part of the century, remembers.

'Sometimes we used to get hold of the cane an' we used to hide him. We used to push 'n up the chimney or put him behind the cupboards. He used to say, "Well, I can't find my cane nowhere." I remember one day he said, "Summerhayes, do you know where the cane is?" "No," I said. "Well," he said, "here's a shilling. Now go down the road an' buy a new one." I done that several times where he couldn't find the other one. He didn't mince no matters about it. He did give it to you hot 'n holy, right up over his shoulders, you know, an' right across that thumb an' it don't half hurt across there, mind. We used to put all sorts on us hands. We used to put our hand in our hair an' put a hair on it so the cane would break. It never did though. Or we'd rub a bit of sugar on there or a bit of resin, you know. None of 'em worked.'

New interpretations of the past can be built from life stories – and you don't have to be a professional historian to have original ideas.

Part three:
Working on
different projects with
different groups

12 Family history

The importance of the oral history approach

There has been a flood of interest in family history in recent years. Family history societies have sprung up all over the country. But many of the people in this field ignore the untapped sources of oral and documentary evidence that surround them in their immediate families, and go rummaging through old parish records instead.

Although it is necessary to visit record offices to research your family history beyond the living memory, the desire to dash back into the distant past as quickly as possible often leads to a neglect of the recollections of old relatives. The information they can provide is not only more accessible than that contained in record offices, it can also be much more interesting and richer in detail.

Oral history, which focuses upon the recent past of our families, can heighten our awareness of ourselves and of the class society in which we live. It can help to foster a greater respect and understanding between people of different ages and preserve the mementoes and memories of our parents and our grandparents, so that they may be seen by and speak to future generations.

An oral history approach to the study of the family also has enormous potential for use with children and young people, especially in schools. It makes possible a child centred approach to the learning of history in which children genuinely create knowledge by themselves to share with their classmates, family and teachers. It encourages a closer relationship between the school and the local community. This chapter explains how to go about studying your family's past and how to organise a project of this type for young people, using an oral history approach.

57

How to make your family tree

Once you have resolved to record and write the history of your family, the first thing that you will probably feel the urge to do, is to begin drawing a family tree. A family tree excites our imagination for many different reasons. It promises to be unique and makes us more conscious of our direct link with the past, of the transience of our own lives. It captures the grand sweep of our family history over many years on a single sheet of paper. This can be passed down through the generations as a precious document in its own right.

You should be able to travel back at least a century using oral evidence alone. But, before you actually begin the search for your ancestors, you should have a clear idea of the people you need to find to fill your family tree and how best to organise the information that you discover about them. The eight rules listed below, together with the two tables, should act as guidelines to help you.

1. Keep an index on loose leaf paper, in which you can note down basic biographical information about each relative to be included on your family tree. Otherwise valuable information may be easily lost or misplaced.

2. Use A4 size paper or large sheets which fold into A4 divisions. A1 will divide into eight A4 sections, A2 divides into four, and A3 divides into two. The advantage of using A4 units is that they provide sufficient space for an outline of a 'trunk' or 'branch' of a family tree, they fit neatly into a loose leaf folder, and they can be easily photocopied.

3. There are two main species of family tree. I have called them the 'trunk' and the 'branch' types. The trunk is particularly suitable for beginners and for use with children embarking on a family history project in school. It is a basic outline of your family's descendants and can easily be drawn on one sheet of A4 size paper (see table on page 59). If you want to save time and trouble, you can duplicate sets of these bare outlines for a class of schoolchildren on a photocopier or banda machine. They can then fill in details of their family history on them.

The branch contains more detailed information on whatever particular line of your family you choose to follow. It could be your father's family, your mother's family, your grandfather's family,

58

TABLE A.

TRUNK OF ALAN TUCKER'S FAMILY

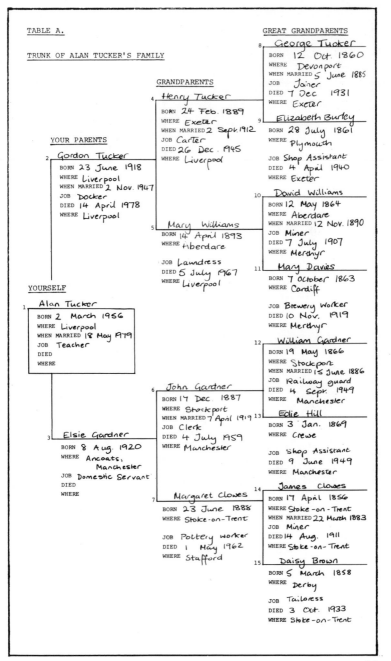

GREAT GRANDPARENTS

8 George Tucker
BORN 12 Oct. 1860
WHERE Devonport
WHEN MARRIED 5 June 1885
JOB Joiner
DIED 7 Dec 1931
WHERE Exeter

9 Elizabeth Burley
BORN 28 July 1861
WHERE Plymouth
JOB Shop Assistant
DIED 4 April 1940
WHERE Exeter

10 David Williams
BORN 12 May 1864
WHERE Aberdare
WHEN MARRIED 12 Nov. 1890
JOB Miner
DIED 7 July 1907
WHERE Merthyr

11 Mary Davies
BORN 7 October 1863
WHERE Cardiff
JOB Brewery Worker
DIED 10 Nov. 1919
WHERE Merthyr

12 William Gardner
BORN 19 May 1866
WHERE Stockport
WHEN MARRIED 15 June 1886
JOB Railway guard
DIED 4 Sept. 1949
WHERE Manchester

13 Edie Hill
BORN 3 Jan. 1869
WHERE Crewe
JOB Shop Assistant
DIED 9 June 1949
WHERE Manchester

14 James Clowes
BORN 17 April 1856
WHERE Stoke-on-Trent
WHEN MARRIED 22 March 1883
JOB Miner
DIED 14 Aug. 1911
WHERE Stoke-on-Trent

15 Daisy Brown
BORN 5 March 1858
WHERE Derby
JOB Tailoress
DIED 3 Oct. 1933
WHERE Stoke-on-Trent

GRANDPARENTS

4 Henry Tucker
BORN 24 Feb. 1889
WHERE Exeter
WHEN MARRIED 2 Sept. 1912
JOB Carter
DIED 26 Dec. 1945
WHERE Liverpool

5 Mary Williams
BORN 14 April 1893
WHERE Aberdare
JOB Laundress
DIED 5 July 1967
WHERE Liverpool

6 John Gardner
BORN 17 Dec. 1887
WHERE Stockport
WHEN MARRIED 7 April 1919
JOB Clerk
DIED 4 July 1959
WHERE Manchester

7 Margaret Clowes
BORN 23 June 1888
WHERE Stoke-on-Trent
JOB Pottery worker
DIED 1 May 1962
WHERE Stafford

YOUR PARENTS

2 Gordon Tucker
BORN 23 June 1918
WHERE Liverpool
WHEN MARRIED 2 Nov. 1947
JOB Docker
DIED 14 April 1978
WHERE Liverpool

3 Elsie Gardner
BORN 8 Aug. 1920
WHERE Ancoats, Manchester
JOB Domestic Servant
DIED
WHERE

YOURSELF

1 Alan Tucker
BORN 2 March 1956
WHERE Liverpool
WHEN MARRIED 18 May 1979
JOB Teacher
DIED
WHERE

59

TABLE B.

BRANCH OF ALAN TUCKER'S FAMILY

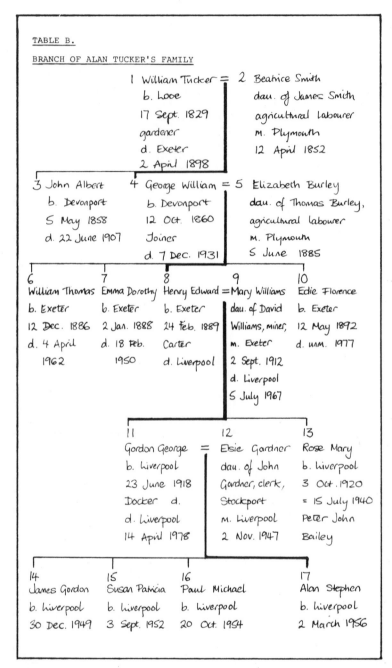

1 William Tucker = 2 Beatrice Smith
b. Looe   dau. of James Smith
17 Sept. 1829   agricultural labourer
gardener   m. Plymouth
d. Exeter   12 April 1852
2 April 1898

3 John Albert   4 George William = 5 Elizabeth Burley
b. Devonport   b. Devonport   dau. of Thomas Burley,
5 May 1858   12 Oct. 1860   agricultural labourer
d. 22 June 1907 Joiner   m. Plymouth
                 d. 7 Dec. 1931   5 June 1885

6   7   8   9   10
William Thomas   Emma Dorothy   Henry Edward = Mary Williams   Edie Florence
b. Exeter   b. Exeter   b. Exeter   dau. of David   b. Exeter
12 Dec. 1886   2 Jan. 1888   24 Feb. 1889   Williams, miner, 12 May 1892
d. 4 April   d. 18 Feb.   Carter   m. Exeter   d. unm. 1977
1962   1950   d. Liverpool   2 Sept. 1912
                                                d. Liverpool
                                                5 July 1967

11   12   13
Gordon George =   Elsie Gardner   Rose Mary
b. Liverpool   dau. of John   b. Liverpool
23 June 1918   Gardner, clerk, 3 Oct. 1920
Docker   d.   Stockport   = 15 July 1940
d. Liverpool   m. Liverpool   Peter John
14 April 1978   2 Nov. 1947   Bailey

14   15   16   17
James Gordon   Susan Patricia   Paul Michael   Alan Stephen
b. Liverpool   b. Liverpool   b. Liverpool   b. Liverpool
30 Dec. 1949   3 Sept. 1952   20 Oct. 1954   2 March 1956

60

and so on (see table on page 60). You have to draw in many different branches before you can paint a complete picture of your family tree. Begin each branch with a new sheet of paper, otherwise they will quickly sprout into a meaningless mass of data.

4. Whenever possible, include basic information about the date and place of birth, date of marriage, occupation, and date and place of death of all your relatives, on your family tree. The information it contains should be clear and self explanatory. Many family trees are confusing or incomprehensible either because too much information has been crammed onto them, or because they have been pruned too drastically.

5. To make your family tree more clear, you should keep husband and wife side by side, and people of the same generation level with each other.

6. Use standard genealogical abbreviations to save space. The most important of these are as follows:

b.	born	dau.	daughter
bapt.	baptised	div.	divorced
bur.	buried	s.	son
d.	died	umn.	unmarried
d. umn.	died unmarried	=	married
d.s.p.	died without children (abbreviation of the Latin – decessit sine prole).		left descendants

I have used some of these abbreviations in the 'branch' table, but for the sake of simplicity, I have avoided them in the 'trunk' table.

7. Always record dates in the form 18 Nov. 1892 and not Nov. 18 1892 or 18.11.1892. The last two forms of dating can be confusing when the numbers are packed tightly together.

8. Give each person a reference number so that you can find them easily and cross reference from one 'branch' to another. The simplest way to do this is to give each chart a letter (A. B. C. etc.), and each person on the chart a number (1, 2, 3 etc.). Thus each person will have one or more codes like A1, B2, and so on, according to how many different branches their name appears on. Number each sheet from top to bottom, and from left to right (see tables on pages 59–60). Finally, insert each person's reference

Timeline chart (ages of family members across historical periods)

Years (right margin): 1882, 1884, 1886, 1888, 1890, 1892, 1894, 1896, 1898, 1900, 1902, 1904, 1906, 1908, 1910, 1912, 1914, 1916, 1918, 1920, 1922, 1924, 1926, 1928, 1930, 1932, 1934, 1936, 1938, 1940, 1942, 1944, 1946, 1948, 1950, 1952, 1954, 1956, 1958, 1960, 1962, 1964, 1966, 1968, 1970, 1972, 1974, 1976, 1978, 1980, 1982, 1984

Monarchs: VICTORIA · EDWARD VII · GEORGE V · EDWARD VIII · GEORGE VI · ELIZABETH II

BOER WAR (1898–1902)

WORLD WAR I (1914–1918)

WORLD WAR II (1939–1945)

11 ME (PAUL LUNN) 1971–
14 MY BROTHER (MIKE LUNN) 1968–
40 MUM (JOAN MULLEN) 1942–
45 DAD (JIM LUNN) 1937–
60 GRAN (MARY MULLEN) 1922–
58 GRANDAD (ALBERT MULLEN) 1920–1978
66 GRAN (EDIE LUNN) 1916–
68 GRANDAD (JOHN LUNN) 1911–1977
85 AUNTY (DAISY LUNN) 1897–

number(s) alongside the biographical information you have collected on them in your index.

Making a retrograph

Young children, especially those of pre-secondary school age, often find it difficult to grasp the idea of the passage of time implied by a family tree. Children have a different concept of time to adults. It is well known that a week can seem like an eternity to a child. To help make them more aware that they have a past which is part of a wider historical process, it is often necessary to use a more clear and vivid visual aid than the family tree, known as a retrograph. This is a chart on which the lives of the child, his/her brothers, sisters, parents, grandparents, and other relatives are drawn as parallel time lines of different lengths. These time lines are visibly correlated with dates listed at the top of the page, and with events which vertically dissect them (see diagram opposite). The most important historical events to include on a retrograph are the major wars, because many people use these as landmarks in their lives. The other events you include is up to you. Get the children to write in on the time lines the age that their relatives were when particular events occurred. Then at the end of each time line get them to insert the age of each person. Many teachers have found that retrographs help children to develop a clearer understanding of the passage of time and of their relationship with the past. Also, most children love making them.

Your autobiography

The first step towards exploring your family's past is to begin writing your own autobiography. It need not be very long, but it is important to write about yourself because it helps you to reflect on your own life experience.

Our own past is usually deeply enmeshed in our family's past, and influenced by their way of life. By writing an autobiography we can develop a deeper awareness of ourselves and a more critical yet sympathetic understanding of our family. This is not only valuable in itself. For it will in turn influence the way we approach researching and writing our family history, helping us to pinpoint key problems and to formulate questions to ask older relatives.

This autobiographical stage is also important for young people as it guides them towards a clearer understanding that they have a past, which is rooted in the history of their family. In addition it encourages them to reflect upon themselves and the society they live in.

Begin writing your life story by making brief notes on the whole outline of your life, listing details such as date of birth, education, marriage, children, changes of address, the different jobs you have had, and so on. If you are younger your outline autobiography will encompass a shorter time scale that will focus on different experiences like changes of school, different boyfriends and girlfriends, and so on. This outline provides a framework from which you can select one period or event in your life at a time to write up or record in detail. A few simple rules: don't get swamped in nostalgia for the past; concentrate on detail and actual incidents rather than generalisations and opinions: and try to give an honest account of the world as you saw it when you were younger – not as you see it now.

How to interview your relatives

Once you have a fairly clear idea of what sort of questions to ask and how to make a family tree, you should begin interviewing your parents, grandparents and other relatives. Use the interviewing and recording techniques described in Part Two. When composing a questionnaire to use with your family, remember that you will need three types of information – genealogical, autobiographical and biographical. It is best to deal with each one separately in the interview.

The genealogical information you need from somebody is their full name and relationship to other members of the family; dates of births, marriages and deaths relating to themselves and to others in the family; and traditions about the family's origins; and details of different occupations and places of residence.

To obtain autobiographical information it helps to divide your questionnaire into different sections, each one focusing upon a particular aspect of life experience before and after marriage. You might include sections on the domestic routine, meals, relationships with parents, family activities, school, leisure, work, religion, politics, and community and class relationships. Model questions on each of these themes are listed in *The Voice of The Past* by Paul Thompson, Oxford University Press (1978).

These questions form a valuable guideline for anybody wishing to obtain autobiographical recollections. You might also encourage your relatives to write their own memoirs. They will probably recall and reflect on events in much more detail if they put pen to paper.

To obtain biographical information about the individuals on your family tree, first ask for a brief outline of their lives. Then build up a series of mini-biographies by asking for further details about their family life, education, work experience, and so on.

When prompted by specific questions relatives often recall moving and remarkable stories that you may have never heard before. This is one of the real excitements of family history, for their stories can help you understand why they have become the people they are.

Projects in schools

Family history projects in schools often produce a wealth of original material which the children can use to write biographies of relatives, draw family trees and retrographs, stage exhibitions and compile radio programmes. If you are helping to organise such a project, it is advisable to restrict the area of study. There is a danger that the unsuspecting young historian may be swamped by a reservoir of untapped memories which every family contains.

A school project is usually most successful if the children confine their investigations to one single ancestral side of the family. Choose the one for which most information is available. This frequently turns out to be the female line, partly because women tend to live longer than men, but also because the preservation has often been more of a female than a male preoccupation in the past.

Shorter, more simple questionnaires should be used when young children are doing the interviews. If you are working with junior school children, it is advisable to restrict the autobiographical section to a few key themes that they can easily identify with, such as clothes, the home and school.

If the children themselves write a short autobiography and then interview parents and grandparents, they should be able to

An oral history project with a Turkish family run by Carry Gorney

make interesting comparisons across three generations, focusing on similarities and differences in dress, relationships with parents and education.

There are several practical problems that may confront a teacher organising a family history project. In most cases they can be solved with little difficulty. First, parents may be suspicious that the school is prying into their private lives. To allay these fears, you should either call a meeting of parents to explain what the project is all about – or write an explanatory note to give to the children to take home. This provides an opportunity for encouraging closer parent-teacher cooperation. Many teachers have commented that parents who had previously shown little interest in their children's school work, became enthusiastically involved in their family history project. They would often help to contact old relatives, arrange interviews and obtain information and photographs.

Although most parents are cooperative, teachers have discovered that in nearly every class one or two children cannot participate because of parental objections, often arising from divorce, illegitimacy or some 'scandal' in the past. Despite the fact that these 'family skeletons' often worry children far less than they do the parents, they should remain firmly locked away, and parental privacy respected. These children could, as an alternative, explore the family history of interesting old people in the locality that they know themselves or that the teacher has previously contacted. This approach can also be used with children who don't have any grandparents living in the locality. But this problem can more often be overcome by letter writing, which can be an equally exciting route into the past. In the multi-ethnic school, for example, children can be encouraged to write to relatives in Bangladesh, the West Indies, Hong Kong, or wherever, to discover more about their family and their culture.

Another difficulty that may arise is obtaining recording equipment. Many children or their families will have access to a portable tape recorder. Those who don't might be supplied with equipment from the school resource centre or from the local teacher's centre. If this proves impossible, children can take notes during the interview. However, this is a difficult and tiring task, and should only be attempted by older children.

Artefacts, documents and photographs

While you are talking to relatives, more often than not they will show you some old documents and photographs or tell you about a family heirloom stored away in the attic. This is always an exciting moment, partly because these artefacts evoke the atmosphere of a previous era in a direct and immediate way, but also because they are often a gold mine of information about the family's past.

Many old people possess collections of old documents and artefacts: apprenticeship indentures, birthday and Christmas cards, diaries, family bibles, letters, picture postcards, school certificates and wartime miscellanea. If you are producing a biographical booklet they may provide vivid illustrative material. Arrange to borrow or copy whatever documents you need. Sometimes you will find relatives so gratified by your interest in their life history, that they will insist that you keep them.

In a school project a particularly interesting document can often be used as a stimulus for a lesson or as part of a classroom exhibition. So can artefacts surviving from the past like old dresses, domestic objects, tools, and family heirlooms – perhaps a Victorian doll passed down through the generations. Old objects that can be handled often hold an irresistible fascination for children.

The collection and study of old photographs is essential for the success of any family history project. Photographs capture the past in vivid detail and give a personal identity to dead ancestors. They are particularly valuable with children, because they help them to identify more closely with old people, and to understand that their grandparents were once young like themselves.

Beyond living memory

It is usually possible to trace your family history back at least three or four generations simply by using oral evidence and documents in the hands of relatives.

If you wish to dig deeper into the past to explore the hidden roots and branches of your family tree, then you will need different tools. You will need a basic knowledge of research methods in public record offices, where you will be sifting through birth, marriage and death certificates, census returns, registers and wills, to discover your ancestors.

Your search may even lead to churchyards, where you will

find yourself deciphering crumbling inscriptions on gravestones which are centuries old.

Learning these skills is perfectly straightforward, but this type of research is often more expensive and time consuming than oral history. An explanation of these techniques is beyond the scope of this book, which aims to concentrate on the 'living' past of the last few generations. If you are interested in pursuing your family history into the distant past, you will find books to guide you in the list of books on page 156.

Many older people surround themselves with their family history. Old portraits, photographs and heirlooms can trigger interesting memories.

13 School

Oral history has the potential to revitalise and transform the way in which schoolchildren learn about the past. It can add a new dimension to teaching in other humanities subjects. Most sections of the book are relevant if you want to organise a school-based project. Information and practical examples for teachers on all aspects of oral history work with children and young people are given.

Ten arguments for oral history

Why give oral history a place in the school curriculum? There are ten key areas which oral history attempts to develop:

1. *Communication skills*, in the spoken and written word.
2. *Social skills* in forming caring and responsible relationships with others outside the school walls.
3. *Artistic and technical skills* in broadcasting, design, film, photography, printing, publishing and recording.
4. *A cooperative approach to learning* – oral history doesn't lend itself to a competitive and individualistic approach.
5. *A critical and creative understanding of evidence* – how to evaluate, interpret and construct arguments on the basis of evidence, rather than memorising a given body of factual information.
6. *An emotional involvement in the past*, through identification with the life experience of others in the locality.
7. *A more integrated approach* to subjects, because it encompasses and makes connections between different subject areas. (This is discussed in more detail later in this section)
8. *A closer relationship between the school and the community* – through oral history a child's parents, grandparents, neighbours, and other members of the local community, can all make a

70

valuable contribution to his or her educational development, and can become directly involved in school projects.

9. *A more understanding relationship between different generations* – by bringing young and old into direct contact, both gain an insight into each other's problems and way of life.

10. *A higher level of awareness of the society in which we live* – from the point of view of ordinary people and oppressed groups, rather than a privileged elite.

It is true that other school subjects aspire to some of these aims. However, oral history can often achieve them more effectively because it has the power to capture the imagination and involvement of children and young people. It is an essentially child-centred and experiential form of learning. It puts kids in real situations with real problems to solve, that are relevant to their interests. Some of this learning is particularly valuable because it takes place in the 'real world' outside the classroom, and away from the direct supervision of the teacher. In a properly organised oral history project, children are genuinely productive and purposeful. They can create things which are of interest and value to

Arran High School children in Scotland learn about an Island way of life now almost vanished.

71

themselves and others – books, exhibitions, radio programmes, and so on.

Oral history projects have been used by pioneering teachers in many schools during the past decade and have produced encouraging and exciting results. What they have achieved is featured in this and other sections of the book (see also Sallie Purkis, *Oral History in Schools*, available from The Oral History Society, Department of Sociology, University of Essex, Colchester CO4 3SQ, for £1 post free).

Some practical problems and how to solve them

There are four main practical problems that will confront teachers who wish to use the oral history approach. They are problems of money, time, organisation and exams. We will look at each in turn, and the possible ways of solving them.

Money

A class set of cassette recorders, equipped with microphones and tapes, will cost around £500. A class set is desirable though not essential for an oral history project. However, £500 represents a large slice out of a school's allowance for resources especially in view of the cuts in educational expenditure. How can such an outlay be justified and obtained?

First, it is advisable to organise a project with a small group using recorders that the kids themselves have brought in. You will probably find several in any class who possess their own recorders and are willing to bring them into school. If this pilot project is seen to be a success, you are on much stronger ground when you come to argue for the purchase of equipment.

Secondly, make it clear that you envisage oral history, not as a one-off novelty, but as an integral part of the school curriculum. If you plan regular projects with different classes throughout the school year, and in subsequent years, you can argue that the equipment will be used extensively, and therefore give good value for money. Also, there is the argument that the equipment enables you to create taped resource material for subsequent school use.

Thirdly, if you are teaching in a secondary school, try to get

Sonya (holding microphone), 'They say you have to be in school to learn things but you can learn outside as well. Like just talking to people about their life, you can learn a lot from that.'

as much support as possible for the project from within your department and in other departments. This should not be too difficult, because oral history projects have considerable potential for interdisciplinary work. They will usually be based in the history department but because they develop communication and social skills, they have close links with the English teacher's concern with literacy. The scope which they offer for autobiographical and biographical work, and dramatisations, brings them shoulder to shoulder with the imaginative side of English teaching. An oral history project will also complement and enrich environmental and geographical studies of the locality which are frequently undertaken by schools. Oral history projects also overlap into the closely related areas of Social Studies and Economics, and they could easily be adapted to provide case studies for these subjects.

Finally, the technical and imaginative skills that an oral history project aims to develop provides a link with the teaching of Art, Design and Photography (if this is taught).

Pointing out this interdisciplinary potential to other depart-

73

ments gives you a double advantage. It makes possible a project which connects different subject areas and draws upon the knowledge and skills of other teachers. Also, it enables you to argue that the outlay on equipment is justifiable because it will have a multiple purpose.

If there is no way that your budget allowance will run to £500 for recorders, or if you need additional funds you can try your Parent-Teachers Association. Because this type of project promises to forge closer links between the school and the community, and because the equipment could be put to many uses you would have a good chance of persuading parents to help raise funds towards it.

Time

Arranging interviews with local people, which in the first instance will probably be the responsibility of the teacher, can be time consuming. So can the other organisational arrangements involved in an oral history project. Is it worth the time, and are there any short cuts which save time?

There is no doubt that launching an oral history project involves a lot of hard work. You should recruit as much help as possible from other teachers, parents and pupils, to get it moving. The school holidays are the best time to make initial arrangements and contacts in the local community.

However, once you have built up a stock of equipment, a reliable network of interviewees and an indexing system, a properly organised project will almost run itself. Things are never as hectic as they are in the first few weeks. The key to success is forging *permanent* relationships with local people who have vivid memories, so that different children and young people can go back to visit them on other projects in the future.

Organisation

Oral history projects involve pupils going out of school into the local community. A teacher might fairly ask, how often? And, is this feasible in terms of the organisation of the school day?

On this type of project a pupil will probably spend less than one fifth of his or her total time outside the classroom. The main reason for going out of school will be to record interviews. Most activities, such as constructing questionnaires, indexing, making

74

radio programmes, transcribing tapes (using earplugs), writing autobiographies and biographies, and so on, will take place in the classroom. Clearly, the more time that is spent in the classroom on the project, the less of an organisational problem it is.

Oral history projects are most easily organised when small groups of pupils are involved. But they are also feasible with whole classes. You can organise projects with children and young people of all ages but the scope has to be more limited with young children. Advice on this and other matters relating to oral history in schools is contained in Sallie Purkis, *Oral History in Schools* (see bibliography).

It should be possible to arrange for a handful of pupils to go out to record interviews each week. One advantage of organising the project in this way, is that you only need a few recorders, because only a few are being used at any one time. Always arrange practice interviews before the pupils go out and do the real thing. Working in pairs they can ask each other questions about their own life histories. They need to be taught how to interview, and also how to use the recording equipment properly.

Before sending pupils out on interviews, it is often a good idea to give them a 'feel' for oral history. You could perhaps invite some old people into the school for the pupils to talk to. You could play recordings of interviews that you have made to your pupils. Or you could use taped radio broadcasts or copies borrowed from local oral history collections. BBC Schools Radio producer Janet Whitaker and myself compiled a series of ten programmes called *People Talking* to stimulate interest and discussion on oral history in the classroom. Each programme contains interesting extracts, most of them focussing on memories of childhood and youth, taken from oral history archives all over the country. The programmes were transmitted in 1981 and 1983 but teachers who missed these broadcasts can buy copies of the tapes from Theatre Projects Services Ltd, 11–13 Neals Yard, Monmouth St, London WC2H 9 JG.

If you are in Scotland, you might consider recording the BBC Schools Radio series *From Scotland's Past*, produced by Marinell Ash, an enthusiastic oral historian. This and future series which are planned will be of interest to teachers working in this field. In recent years Scottish schools have been encouraged to embark on oral history projects of their own, to send in tapes to the BBC and to compete for prizes offered by the Saltaire Society and publishers W. Chambers. This has stimulated some excellent work by pupils. If you wish to become involved in this project, further information can be obtained from The Saltaire Society, Saltaire House, 13 Atholl Crescent, Edinburgh EH3 8HA.

Exams

The curriculum in the upper part of the secondary school is geared to a competitive examination system. Do the constraints inherent in this system mean that oral history projects are unworkable in the upper school?

The answer to this question is an emphatic no. In the past decade there have been important initiatives to decentralise the examination system, and to give it greater flexibility and responsiveness to pupil and school needs. Oral history projects in the upper school can take advantage of these changes. Their presence in the curriculum will encourage further changes away from the traditional, standardised and examination based forms of assessment which have for so long hindered cooperative, creative and experimental learning in the secondary school.

The Mode 111 CSE gives individual schools the opportunity to exercise some control over the content of courses, allows some continuous assessment, and the setting and marking of examinations by the schools themselves. Oral history projects can take full advantage of this flexibility. They should also exploit the changes in policy of GCE 'O' and 'A' level examining boards, which are increasingly offering optional projects or open ended local history questions on their papers. The AEB (Associated Examining Board) has led the field in this area.

Ideas for life history projects in schools

1. Your school. If your school is more than fifty years old, there should be a mine of information on its history for you to dig into. There will be old school attendance registers, log books and punishment books. There will be the memories of former pupils and teachers still living in the area. Many of these people will have old school photographs, attendance certificates and school reports.

You might find that some of the old pupils you speak to are

76

the parents, grandparents or other relatives of present day pupils. This makes the project more exciting by adding an extra dimension of family history to it. School history booklets are often bestsellers in the locality, especially if you can produce one to coincide with the school's centenary.

One word of warning. Don't let nostalgia and loyalty to your school prevent you from criticising its teaching methods and organisation in the past. For two examples of school histories enlivened by the memories of old pupils, see, *Fleet School Centenary Book* (1978) and *Llanhon School: A Century and More of Education* (1978).

2. Childhood and youth. The great advantage of a project focussing on childhood and youth is that because every adult has been a child and youth, they are all potential interviewees. This makes it an ideal subject in a new town or housing estate where the residents and their children have no shared local history. Also, by concentrating on this period in life, we can reach as far back into the past as possible with the human memory.

There is much potential here for the younger generation to compare and contrast their own experiences of growing up with those of older generations. Get the kids to focus on whatever aspects of childhood and youth interest them most. It could be relationships with parents, street games, clothes and fashion, courting, and so on.

One particularly successful project focusing on memories of youth was devised by Carry Gorney on a housing estate in Milton Keynes in 1977. The scheme was constructed around the title 'Sweet Sixteen'. It aimed to bring people beyond their front doors, and to encourage them to get to know each other by sharing experiences and working together. On a street by street basis the residents of Beanhill Estate were interviewed and interviewed each other, on their personal memories of life at sixteen. These led onto street parties, street newspapers, a cabaret, and the making of a video tape which was screened several times by Channel 40. Many residents invited families from out of town to watch the screenings. The full story of the 'Sweet Sixteen' project is to be published in a forthcoming Inter-Action book.

3. Class inequality. This is a subject of fundamental social and political importance, which is often distorted or disguised in school books and broadcasts. Oral history can help contribute

*Participants in the Sweet Sixteen project run by Carry Gorney
in Milton Keynes.*

social awareness, for class inequality can be graphically illustrated
by comparing and contrasting the life histories of local people
from different class backgrounds. This type of social history
could provide young people with a valuable understanding of the
class nature of our society.

4. Oppressed groups. An oral history approach to the position
of oppressed groups such as women and racial minorities in

78

twentieth century Britain, which explores their family, school and work experiences, would be likely to develop a sharper awareness of sexist and racist elements.

One recent example of this was a project on the causes and effects of racism undertaken by English teacher and writer, Chris Searle, with his 12 to 14 year old children in a multi-racial East London school. Through autobiographies, poems and plays, children of different nationalities were encouraged to speak and write about their experiences of racism. Contemporary experiences were combined with an exploration of the struggle against racism in local history and in the Third World, to capture 'the world in a classroom'. As a result the children not only produced some moving and imaginative work but more important, they were able to understand more clearly the racist undercurrents in our society.

5. A single street or neighbourhood, preferably one in which a number of children in your class live, can often provide the basis for an interesting oral history project, with which pupils can readily identify. Changes, for example in housing, local amenities and life styles, can often be focused upon in clear and vivid detail by telescoping local history in this way.

Two excellent examples of this type of study are, Jerry White, 'Campbell Bunk: A Lumpen Community in London between the Wars', in *History Workshop Journal*, Autumn 1979 (a powerful description and analysis of a rough street in North London that resisted police control, written by a socialist historian). And, *The Island: The Life and Death of an East End London Community*, published by Centerprise, 1979 (a moving social history of an isolated square of five streets built in 1871 and demolished a century later, produced by a community publishing group).

6. A local industry or occupation. Many industries spawned by the first industrial revolution, such as coal mining, textiles and heavy engineering, are either slowly dying or are being transformed by new technology. It is crucial to preserve a record of the lives of those who laboured for long hours and low wages in factories, mills and mines, before death and the destruction of documents and artefacts, deprive us of most of the evidence.

The shop floor culture, the skills of the workforce, and their bitter conflicts with employers, are not only interesting in them-

79

selves as part of our cultural heritage but also teach us important political lessons about the organisation of work in an unequal society.

The Manchester Studies Department at Manchester Polytechnic, has recently produced an innovatory teaching pack called *Hurrah for Life in the Factory*. It is based on seventy five interviews recorded with people who have vivid memories of working in the cotton mills before the First World War. Each pack contains cassettes and transcripts of extracts taken from the interviews, plus facsimiles of contemporary photographs, cartoons, documents, and background information for teachers, together with suggestions for using the pack in the classroom. The pack has been well received in Lancashire schools, and has stimulated children and teachers to embark on oral history research of their own. If your school wishes to use the pack, contact Manchester Studies Unit, Cavendish House, Cavendish Street Manchester M15 6BG.

7. Folklore and rural crafts, make perfect subjects for oral history projects. This type of project is tailor made for village schools, which have the raw material on their doorstep. As the mass media, urbanisation and new technologies and farming methods rapidly change the face of life in the countryside, it is important that we preserve a record of what is left of the traditional life style of the older generations. Such a project can help to foster a concern for the rural way of life, not only as part of our heritage, but as a 'living' culture. What remains must be protected from the ravages of entrepreneurs and planners. To whet your appetite for oral history in this field, read Ronald Blythe, *Akenfield: Portrait of an English Village*, Penguin (1976) and George Ewart Evans, *Ask the Fellows who Cut the Hay* Faber (1956) and *Where Beards Wag All: The Days that We Have Seen* Faber (1975).

Folklore and rural crafts have provided the basis for one very successful school oral history project known throughout the United States as 'Foxfire'. It is organised by Eliot Wigginton at Nacoochee High School, Rabun Gap, in the mountains of Georgia. Pupils record details of local crafts like log cabin building, and quilt and straw mattress making, recalled by old people in the neighbourhood. They often give the pupils a practical demonstration of the craft. Pupils also record centuries-old local customs and beliefs which surround childbirth, sickness and death. Their research regularly appears in the school magazine, and anthologies have been published in a series of six *Foxfire* books (Anchor Press/Doubleday) which have together sold over a million copies.

8. War, is a subject that intrigues many children and young people. Here is an opportunity to make the study of this subject more immediate and moving, by using the memories and mementoes of local old people involved in the First and Second World Wars. You might focus upon life in the trenches or in munitions factories in the First World War, or Dunkirk, D.Day, the Blitz, the evacuation of children or the Home Guard in the Second World War. Alternatively you might decide to document the resistance to the military, expressed in conscientious objection, mutinies and soldier's strikes. Or you might explore the wave of radical thought amongst servicemen and women during the Second World War, which, among other things culminated in the Labour victory of 1945 and the development of a welfare state. There is enormous scope here for projects using oral evidence.

9. Whatever is interesting to you and your class, is always a good subject to study! The advantage of oral history is that you have such a wide choice. Studies which focus on local trends in clothing, food, housing and leisure or politics, crime, religion, sex and unemployment, are just a few of the many possibilities that might appeal to you and your class. For a comprehensive bibliography of oral history articles and books see Paul Thompson, *The Voice of the Past* Oxford University Press (1978). This will give you plenty of other ideas for projects.

10. Just for fun. Ask people abouty funny incidents that they remember from the past. Most of us have a fund of stories, often involving accidents, misunderstandings, personal disasters and practical jokes which we look back on and laugh at. This would make an ideal 'quick' project in which only short interviews were required.

14 Literacy

Oral history and literacy

There are around two million semi or non literate people in Britain today of differing ages (excluding children below reading age). Some can be found in remedial classes in schools, some in adult literacy groups. Many more are too frightened to admit their difficulties in reading and writing to anyone. Some are first or second generation immigrants who find the English language a problem (but may be fluent in another language). Others are people born and bred in Britain who have gone through the treadmill of state schooling, learning little or nothing. The overwhelming majority are working class.

Oral history can offer these people a key with which to unlock their literacy problems and their potential for emotional and intellectual development. It can heighten their critical capacities and give them a sense of self respect and solidarity with others in a similar position to themselves. Such an awareness is essential if they are to overcome their isolation and lonliness and withstand the contempt and ridicule commonly directed against them. An oral history project adjusted to the needs of these people can restore to them their fundamental right to read and write.

Alternative activities

Because oral history is based essentially upon the spoken word, those who find the written word difficult can participate in this type of project without experiencing failure and inadequacy. Mastery of many of the activities involved in an oral history project such as recording interviews and editing tapes, does not depend on having reading and writing skills. They are open to all. When success is achieved by literacy students it not only promotes their self esteem and their powers of self expression. It also stimulates their interest in a project so that when they come to approach those aspects of oral history which do involve reading and writing, they do so with a renewed appetite for learning.

Autobiography and language experience

The most important aim of an oral history project involving literacy students should be the production of autobiographies and writing which expresses personal experience. During the past decade a number of literacy schemes and writer's workshops have taken radical initiatives in this direction, by developing a method widely referred to as 'language experience'. As the name suggests, this involves drawing on the language and experience of each individual student. There are four main steps in the language experience method.

1. The starting point is a small group conversation or discussion about some aspect of personal experience. It might focus upon family life, schooling, leisure activities, work, or whatever. To stimulate the conversation, family photographs or other visual aids might be used.
2. The tutor records the conversation on tape and later transcribes a few interesting extracts from what was said.
3. At the next session the students attempt to read a short typescript containing their words.
4. The grammar, language and ideas contained in the extract are discussed. The speaker is encouraged to improve the clarity of what he or she said, by editing the original version, with the tutor's assistance.

Follow up work can take a variety of forms, dependent upon the stage in reading and writing that the student has reached. This new approach to literacy is explained in depth in a pioneering book by adult literacy tutor Jane Mace, *Working with Words: Literacy Beyond School*, (Writers and Readers Publishing Cooperative, 1979). Many of the suggestions this book contains on the language experience method, could be adapted for use in the classroom with 'remedial' groups.

There are four main advantages for literacy students in this method. First, if the text is in their own language, their own rhythms of speech, and if it is about people and subjects they are familiar with, their chances of reading these words are greatly increased. The process of reading and writing becomes more comprehensible as they realise the close connections between the spoken and the written word.

Secondly, the reflection upon personal life experience encouraged by this method, stimulates the development of a higher level of self and social awareness. This is particularly the case if tutors encourage their students to think of illiteracy and the injustices which follow from it, in terms of social inequality (and not personal inadequacy).

Thirdly, this method helps to motivate the students by giving them greater confidence in themselves and their views. When people who have come to think of themselves as fools and failures realise that somebody is interested in what they have to say, it gives them a new determination to break through to literacy.

Fourthly, this method helps literacy students to think of themselves as producers as well as consumers of the written word. The importance of this is explained in the following section.

Writing and publishing: communication between equals

Those involved in the new approach to literacy not only encourage their students to write. They also believe that the life stories of the students should be published. This commitment to publication shows a determination to overcome the feelings of inferiority and isolation that literacy students have traditionally endured. These feelings are overcome when a student sees his or her ideas and words in print or when they read about experiences and problems they share, expressed in the words of somebody like themselves. This is communication between equals. And it is of essential importance in fostering the confidence and collective consciousness of literacy students.

Many of the initiatives in publishing the work of literacy students have come from groups affiliated to the Federation of Worker Writers and Community Publishers, especially the Write First Time Collective. *Write First Time* was first published in 1975, and has a circulation of about 6,000 per issue. It is a paper containing articles by men and women, some of them learning within hospitals and prisons, about a wide range of working class

84

experience. Since 1977 a committed editorial group of literacy workers has travelled to different parts of the country to produce each issue in collaboration with a different set of students and tutors. Other groups in the federation like Centerprise in Hackney and Commonword in Manchester, also regularly publish booklets containing writings by literacy students. Most of them are autobiographical.

Speaking to each other in print

In our society the voices of the non literate are rarely listened to. But they have much to say of interest and importance. Three examples to illustrate the range of writing produced by literacy students follow.

First, a short piece by Terry Collins, which appeared in a recent issue of Write First Time. It was written as an angry response to being made redundant. The first idea, which was two sentences long, was typed up and duplicated. Then everybody in the group discussed the issue and Terry added to it. Below is his final draft. He was then given some advice on spelling and setting before the piece appeared in the form printed on the following page. You will notice that the lines of print are broken at points of

This man said I was to slow
For him so I at wark so I told
the pro lady about him and
He thealad with the sack he
He sent my mother and dad a
Letter so we went see the disabled
Lady and she telephona him
and she was ver angey about
it I was we when pushed
out of the door like crimihal
and could not see to say anything
about it. but acording to
His set his time and emotion.
man: made redundant

Made redundant

by T. A. P. Collins

This man at work
told the boss that I was too slow for him.
He sent my mother and dad a letter
so we went to see the Disabled Resettlement Officer.
I told her that he threatened me with the sack.
She telephoned him as she was very angry about it.

Me and this other boy, we were pushed around,
out of the door like criminals
and could not say anything about it.
But according to him, the time and motion man,
I was too slow.

He made me redundant.
I had been there eleven years and nine months.

sense within the sentence. This is a device used in many recent adult literacy publications, to make phrases easier to read and understand.

Next, as an example of the writing of young people, here is an extract from the autobiography of Mohammed Elbaja, a former pupil at Shoreditch School. He learnt to express himself fluently in written English by writing about his memories of life in Morocco before being brought to Britain by his parents. His life story was first published in a booklet by his school, and it subsequently appeared in a collection of young people's auto- biographies *Our Lives* ILEA English Centre (1979). In the following extract he describes the agony of his family on the day his father boarded a boat in Tangiers to look for work in Scotland.

> We got off the coach in Tangiers and it was the afternoon about three o'clock. The boat was leaving at four o'clock. We all carried the bags and my father carried the suitcase. My father's face was white and he didn't know what to do next.

> He started to kiss us and he was crying like a little boy. I have never seen my father crying like that. We were all crying. And they were calling the people to go to their places on the boat, but we wouldn't let our father go. It seemed a horrible day.

> Then our father went on the ship and he went on the deck. He got out his handkerchief and started waving with it. The ship left and he was still waving. We were all crying.

My mother said to me, 'Come son, he will come back some day', and I told that to my little brothers. We went to the coach station to catch the coach. We got on the coach and left Tangiers. It was horrible going on the coach, all silent, none of us were talking.

We went home. My mother was still crying. My grandma came to our house and she was crying as well. The day passed, and thank God it did.

The next morning was a morning without a father. He was still travelling because it would take him about five days to get to Scotland.

LIFE WITHOUT A FATHER

A life without a father. I know some people have not missed their fathers. Well I think it is horrible. Our mother bought us a lot of things to play with and things to make us happy, but she had no-one to make her happy. She just put everything in her heart.

Finally here is an extract taken from an extraordinary book, *Dobroyed* by Leslie Wilson (published by Commonword, 61 Bloom St, Manchester M1 3LY, price £1.25). It is the story of one year in Dobroyed approved school. It is the result of years of struggle by the author to overcome his lack of conventional literacy skills, and put down as accurately and honestly as possible his experiences there.

Leslie's unconventional style of writing gives emotional power to his unconventional life story and his resistance to authority. As the publishers point out, his personality and unique vision would be lost if his language was taken away from him and 'corrected'. This is how the book begins:

'Have you aney-thing to say before we pass sentence?' said one of the three magistrates.

'Yes your hanner, I do have something to say. Something to say about my life. Everything I'v tried to make better of has drifted apart without warning, and my lost hopes leading me to fear,' I began in a best performance of manner, and naw slowly to-words the magistrates desck.

'I don't want my probation officer telling you I need help. I don't need help. I need a finall chance to proove to you I can fite this unfortunet, and proove that I will. I want to start work and feel proud of saing to my probation officer I am continuing life respectidelly. This is the time I no I can proove something big on livving the way I no. Pleace your worships, I ask you for the finall chance, beleave me you honnor,' I finnished loudly in such effort.

'Yes, allrite, you can sit your-selth dawn naw you'v explaind your point,' said the middle magistrait in a kind of low wonndering way.

It was naw time for the silence wispering.

'Would you please stand,' he spoke.

'Naw we are giving you a chance by sending you to an aprooved school,' he said carmly. All at once, I felt miselth going into a num sence then deeper, untill I felt to week to move.

'We are naw sighning an approoth school order.'

I changed to a dizzy feeling with the surrounding of people then two officer who walked before me, by the one normal grip on my sleeves, and a feelling of anouth strengh to get through the door, along the marble path of the continues corridors leading deeper and deeper into the waiting room of locks, bars, and keys. I fourt of nothing untill hearing the ecoing sound of lock and keys being rackled again into the prison doors.

The Arbroath History Project sponsored by the Manpower Services Commission creating a valuable oral history archive in Scotland.

15 Unemployed youth

Mass youth unemployment is one of the most fundamental social and political problems of our day. To maintain control over the lives of young people, to provide some work opportunities and to prevent an increase of dissatisfaction and disorder on the streets, a lot of money is being pumped into state sponsored schemes for unemployed youth like the Youth Training Scheme and the Community Programme. Although these schemes offer no long term solution to the problems of unemployed youth, and many employers exploit them as a source of cheap labour, an oral history project could use the money provided by the government to offer genuinely creative and socially purposeful opportunities. Any individual or organisation can run a scheme. If your idea is well thought out there is a good chance that the Manpower Services Commission (MSC), the controlling body for schemes involving unemployed youth, will accept it. MSC funds provide opportunities for oral history projects attached to community centres, libraries, museums, schools, universities, welfare organisations, and so on. Although you don't get paid anything yourself as the sponsor of a scheme, the MSC foot all the wage bills, and make a contribution towards capital costs. This section explains how to get funding for such a project, and how to organise it.

Planning the project – eight targets

The first stage in planning this type of project is to decide upon specific targets to aim at. The achievement of these goals must clearly benefit both the project workers and the local community, as these are two of the main criteria used by the MSC when deciding whether or not to finance a scheme.

To ensure that your project fulfills these pre-conditions, that it attracts a broad body of local support, and that its programme of activities is varied enough to hold the imagination of the project workers, it is advisable to formulate at least two or three main aims. Eight suggested targets are listed below. Many of them are complementary and inter-related – the material generated in one area could be used simultaneously in another.

1. Create an oral history archive/resource centre in your local reference library, comprising taped interviews and transcripts, and copies of the autobiographies, documents and photographs you have collected.

2. Produce oral history booklets and broadsheets with a strong local interest and relevance.

3. Provide resources for learning for local schools. These might comprise an edited selection of your most outstanding tapes and transcripts, life history booklets, and interesting documents and photographs. You could aim to produce a teaching pack that contains all of these items, together with notes suggesting ways in which teachers and pupils might make use of the material. Some teacher's centres have equipment available to reproduce large quantities of booklets and tapes, and would be likely to co-operate in a plan to produce and distribute such material to local schools.

4. Stage exhibitions of the photographs and documents that you collect, accompanied by edited tapes of interviews, in local arts and community centres, schools, libraries, museums, and so on.

5. Form a travelling group which performs plays, gives illustrated talks and readings, and exhibits slide shows, based on the material that you collect and create.

6. Compile a series of programmes using edited extracts from interviews, to be broadcast on local radio.

7. Make a video programme about some aspect of local history.

8. Perform an enabling role, promoting, organising and transporting people to local life history events. (For example, arranging for groups of old people to visit and talk to children in school).

Enhancing employment prospects

The most essential requirement in order for your project to qualify for MSC funding, is that it must try to enhance the future job prospects of the people it employs. Project organisers aren't expected to find jobs for former workers when their scheme ends – an almost impossible task given the present unemployment. But they are expected to provide work which develops knowledge and skills that are in demand on the job market.

There are several ways of doing this. First, most projects will involve a considerable typing workload. You could arrange for your workers to enrol and attend a half or one day a week release course at a local college, leading to a RSA typing certificate. Despite the development of computer based technology, the ability to type remains an important asset when seeking a clerical position or secretarial job. Argue this point strongly to MSC and remind them of all the typing experience that your project workers will be getting. If you can train your project workers in the use of word processors, this would further enhance their employment prospects and could make your project even more likely to attract MSC funding.

Secondly, all projects involve keeping accounts, calculating tax returns and paying wages. If you arrange for these duties to be shared on a rota basis, then you can fairly claim that you are providing a basic training for all your project workers in the skills needed to be an accounts clerk.

Third, you can argue that your project will develop useful technical skills. The coding, storage and retrieval of tapes involves the understanding of methods commonly used in commercial organisations. The transcription of taped material is of direct relevance to learning office skills. And the operation of recording equipment provides a valuable introduction to the efficient use of technical equipment in offices.

Fourth, depending on the precise targets that you have set for your project, you can argue that the work experience you are offering will increase your workers' opportunities of finding full time employment in resource centres, radio stations, libraries, museums, adult literacy schemes, and in community work with the aged.

Finally your project will develop self confidence and communication skills which will help increase a young person's chances of obtaining and holding a job.

Finding a base

Once you are clear in your mind about the aims of your project, the next stage is to find a base for operations. One room will usually suffice. If space is tight, and only a few project workers are likely to be involved, you may be able to squeeze everybody into part of a large room or working area used by other people. The MSC tend to be rather suspicious if the project base is a private flat or house, and prefer it to be attached to an official organisation. Also if you use somebody's home as a base, you invite the legal and tax problems of it being seen as a 'business premises'. For prospective organisers who are members of staff of colleges, schools, libraries, museums, radio stations or teacher's centres, or who work for other recognised community groups, there should be little problem. Most buildings should have a few square yards of spare space or a junk filled corner that can be easily cleared and transformed into a project base.

If you have no access to a suitable working area, then you will have to canvass the local organisations who are most likely to benefit from your proposed scheme to give you some space. In fact, I was in this position in early 1979 when, as a student, I launched the Bristol People's Oral History Project for unemployed young people in the area. I persuaded the Avon Resources For Learning and Development Unit to provide us with the use of a room for one year on the condition that we supplied them with edited tapes that they could distribute to local schools. They gave us much valuable advice and support, as I'm sure many other educational and cultural organisations would, if their co-operation was sought in this type of venture.

Applying for a MSC grant

There are two types of schemes which would consider funding your oral history project: the Youth Training Scheme and the Community Programme. Under the Youth Training Scheme 16 and 17 year old school leavers are funded for a one year programme of work at the rate of £25 per week. The Community

92

Programme recruits men and women aged between 18 and 24 years old who have been unemployed for over 6 months, and those over 25 who have been unemployed for 12 out of the last 15 months. Exceptions to these rules are permitted when, for example, a skilled worker essential to the success of the project is required and there are no suitable people amongst the long term unemployed. The wages of project workers on the Community Programme must reflect the local rate for the job, and the overall payments to all the workers on a project must average out at no more than £60 per person. National Insurance payments are paid over and above this by the MSC. In either scheme you can employ as many people as you like – the most manageable would be one recruiting between three and eight people.

When applying for a grant it is best to include written confirmation of local support for your scheme. So, if and when somebody offers to provide you with a base for your project or additional financial support, ask them to put it in writing. Then collect as many letters of support as possible. If you are attached to be a recognised institution you may only need a couple to make your case. However, if you don't possess this badge of respectability it is advisable to collect ten or so letters of support to persuade the authorities that your project would be workable and worthwhile. The greater the support you arouse the greater the chances are that your project will win financial backing.

The major targets to aim at are people in positions of responsibility in educational and cultural organisations – museum curators, reference librarians, archivists, history lecturers in universities or colleges, schoolteachers, wardens in teachers centres, secretaries of local history societies, and so on. Contact these people by phone or letter or arrange to meet them face to face. Try to convince them that your project deserves their support. In my experience they are usually very co-operative, and can be easily persuaded to write an enthusiastic letter of support, particularly if your project promises to benefit them, directly or indirectly. You must write to your local MSC office for sponsor's forms on which you have to fill in a detailed account of the scheme's aims, costing and work programme. The MSC give these forms to any prospective project organiser, along with information on how to complete them. They will inform you what rates of pay your project workers are entitled to, and advise you on any other administrative arrangements you may be uncertain about.

Include your letters of support when returning these forms. If you have strong local support for your scheme and have planned it in reasonable detail, then the last stage – a short interview with the MSC representative – should be merely a formality.

Additional financial support

Although the MSC pay the wages of project workers, they only make a nominal contribution towards the capital and running costs on their schemes. The current rate on the Community Programme is a maximum of £440 per project and worker per year, whether full time or part time. Although it pays to have a few part timers on a scheme simply because they boost up the total amount of operating costs you can claim overall, these funds are still barely adequate to pay for the recording equipment, tapes and typewriters, paper, display materials and travelling expenses that are needed in this type of project. If you are not careful you may find yourself a few hundred pounds out of pocket by the time the scheme winds up. Of course, if you have access to an organisation with these resources, then this problem of purchasing expensive equipment does not present itself.

However, if more funding is needed you can seek financial assistance from the organisations who are the proposed beneficiaries of your scheme. After all, you are providing them with free labour and free materials. In 1979 I managed to persuade the Avon County Reference Library to loan equipment and buy tapes for the Bristol People's Oral History Project in return for the completed recordings and transcripts, which they could use as the basis of a local sound archive. Many libraries and teachers centres are interested in developing this type of oral history archive at the moment, and may loan equipment or make a contribution towards the costs you incur, in exchange for assistance in such a project.

Recruitment, training and finance

Once the scheme has been approved advertisements for the positions on it will appear in local job centres.

On every scheme you are allowed a certain proportion of 'supervisors' to 'assistants'. On an oral history project funded by the Community Programme, it can help to recruit trained teachers, history graduates, or people with relevant experience – which need not include formal qualifications – to the supervisory positions. There are many such unemployed people at the moment. The application of their knowledge and skills should ensure that your project gets off to a smooth start and is organised in an efficient manner. Also they will help teach the younger, more inexperienced workers, techniques of interviewing, transcribing, indexing and so on.

For the first few weeks of the project you will need to work closely with them, purchasing equipment, organising training and planning activities, etc. When choosing your supervisors it is useful to have somebody with access to a car. If somebody can offer you this as well as some form of historical expertise, then you should take their application very seriously – they could prove to be invaluable.

Although it pays to play it safe and choose a supervisor with good qualifications and experience, you can afford to be more flexible and experimental when recruiting other project workers. People with little or no formal qualifications often possess a real flair for this type of work, especially the interviewing and recording.

There is no reason why anyone – to the extent that they are enthusiastic about the project – should be excluded from joining it. And despite the fact that MSC pay supervisors at a higher rate than other workers and expect them to perform a managerial role, you do not have to run a scheme rigidly along these lines. You can organise it on a more equal basis, if you have a mind to.

The final matter that requires careful consideration during the early stages of a project is finance. If you are attached to an official organisation, the MSC will normally pay your worker's wages through its accounts office. But if you do not have such connections then you must open up a separate bank account under the name of the project.

Right from the start you must keep accounts, noting down all payments and receipts, otherwise the obligatory audit at the end of the scheme may prove to be catastrophic and costly, especially for you, because you will have to make good any outstanding debts. The MSC staff offer much useful advice and assistance in

An exhibition mounted by the Manchester Studies Unit.

these matters. If you are totally ignorant about cash books and tax returns it pays to read a Teach Yourself Accounts book or do a course, before the project begins. Don't be tempted to spend the lion's share of your capital and running costs within the first few weeks of operations, in the hope that the project will attract financial support from somewhere as it gains momentum. It probably won't, and you will end up footing most of the bills.

The day to day organisation of activities will vary according to the precise nature of your project and the targets that you have set yourself. If you build a sound structure in the initial stages, then it should virtually run itself.

What others have done

Several oral history projects involving unemployed young people have been organised in recent years. Although all of them have had to cope with minor administrative, financial and staffing problems, they have been highly successful overall.

The most outstanding scheme is the one which revolves around the Manchester Studies Unit of Manchester Polytechnic, organised by Bill Williams and Audrey Linkman. Manchester Studies was established in 1974 and now has approximately 25 members, most of whom are externally financed. One of their main sources of income has been the MSC. Amongst their many achievements are the creation of a huge local sound, photographic and film archive, regular exhibitions for local people and a valuable teaching pack for Lancashire schools. Their work is mentioned elsewhere in the book, and is described in detail in an article by Bill Williams and Audrey Linkman, 'Recovering the People's Past: The Archive Rescue Programme of Manchester Studies', in *History Workshop No. 8* (Autumn 1979).

One project which recruited teenagers was '*Our Working Lives:* Life and Labour in Carlisle 1900–1939', which was set up by Sue Bruley at Carlisle Museum from Autumn 1981 to the summer of 1982. Although there were problems on the project, some of them caused by the inexperience of the young inter-viewers, it was overall a huge success. Here is an extract from Sue's summary of the scheme.

'It was difficult to find a suitable supervisor, but by October (1980) a woman had been appointed. Unfortunately she had not lived in Carlisle long, nor had she any historical training. However, as a teacher with an outgoing personality she was able to get on well with the team. She had a couple of weeks for background reading, preparation of classes on social and industrial history for the project workers, and to make preliminary contacts before the team of sixteen to eighteen year olds was appointed. They started work in November. Before interviewing began the supervisor gave background classes to the workers, and they had a chance to get used to the cassette recorders.

Day to day running of the project was carried out by the supervisor. My role was advisory and supervisory. The team was encouraged to read up subjects relevant to individual interviews. Research on local newspapers was also carried out from time to time. Chapters from Paul Thompson's *The Voice of the Past* were prescribed reading. A small library was assembled for the team's office.

It took a long time to establish a steady stream of potential respondents. We found Carlisle people rather shy and somewhat suspicious of the project. But the quality of the tapes improved as members of the team grew more confident in dealing with this. All the project workers showed great enthusiasm for the project. However, I did feel that their lack of experience was a disadvantage. They found interviewing quite a tiring business and many of the interviews are only forty minutes long. Sometimes a follow up visit was made. The end result is an archive of some seventy tapes covering a wide variety of trades, industries and occupations in Carlisle. We were very pleased that one of the girl's experience as an interviewer during the project was directly responsible for her getting a job in a junior position at the local newspaper.

All the kids seemed to enjoy the work and found the experience and the 'social skills' training useful. They could see for themselves an end result of their labours in the exhibition which three of the team helped to mount. About half the photographs used in the exhibition came from respondents and contacts. Members of the team staffed an enquiries table during the exhibition, when many more photographs were handed in by local people. Up to two hundred people per day visited the exhibition, a high number for the time of year. A very high proportion were local people, some of whom hadn't been near the museum for thirty years.

16 Old people

Their unrealised potential

There are almost eight million men and women over the age of sixty-five living in Britain today. The proportion of aged people to the rest of the population is likely to increase in future years. These vast numbers of elderly people, who today live much longer than in previous centuries, are often seen as dependent, deprived of essential faculties by advancing years, and a drain on the resources of the community. Old people are treated as second class citizens. Old age, infirmity and death are a source of deep shame and fear for many people. Even welfare institutions, which claim to act in the interests of the elderly, to some extent manufacture the dependency and passivity of their clients. In short, many old people are robbed of a useful role in our society.

Oral history can do something to change this view of old people, and their inferior view of themselves. Old people possess a rich accumulation of experience, knowledge and skills. It should be spread around the local community, not locked away and left to vegetate. Oral history is one area where they have much to contribute. When their knowledge is harnessed on an oral history project, they should not be viewed as passive sources of information, to be forgotten as soon as the interview is over. Rather, they should be encouraged to play a permanent and important role in the initiation and organisation of projects.

All professional and voluntary organisations involved with old people – community clubs, day centres, education classes, geriatric wards, residential homes, street warden schemes, welfare organisations, and so on – have a vital part to play in such projects. A determined effort in this direction could lead to real progress in increasing the independence, status, and opportunities available to old people. It could enrich the quality of life of the

A photograph brings back memories in a Help the Aged reminiscence group.

local community, and help to eliminate divisive ageist and generational conflict within it. This section will look briefly at some of the ways forward, and at the achievements of some groups working in this field.

Self-directed groups

All the activities described in the other sections of the book – making radio programmes, publishing books, staging exhibitions, and so on – are well within the grasp of groups of elderly people. In the last few years some important initiatives have been taken by individuals and groups working with the elderly, to promote such activities. I want to focus upon two such initiatives.

First, I want to look at the work of Alison Mantle in setting up an oral history project involving old and young people in Lewisham in 1979. Alison worked for Task Force, an organisation concerned with the welfare of elderly people in London, which is largely run by volunteers. She arranged with the Lewisham School History Department, for a group of elderly people, The Friends of Lewisham School Senior Citizens Club, to meet each week at the school in order to form a teaching pack made up of tapes and slides, which could be used by the pupils. ·

The project revolved around making recordings of the group members' personal experiences and memories of World War II. Some of the topics discussed were 'The Rise of Moseley and the Blackshirts', 'Air Raids and Local Bombings', 'Concentration Camps', and 'The Position of Women During the War'. Although Alison felt in retrospect that the old people should have exercised more control over the organisation of the project, it was very successful. Her description of what happened, vividly illustrates how this type of project can 'take off', and lead to links between different groups, which were not originally planned.

'Before each weekly session, I did some preparation in which I thought of various questions about the general area under discussion. Usually these just served to get the session going, as we then regularly got side tracked by people's interesting experiences. However, it was always I who started the session. I was the person with the tape machine, co-ordinating to a large extent who spoke when. This role should have been shared among the group, possibly with a different person each week. Within the Lewisham group, several of them would, I think, have done this with some encouragement and support.

Most of the time we found it easier if the discussion was quite ordered, with myself asking one particular person to make their contribution. When we did otherwise, people forgot about the tape and regularly talked across each other, or various different conversations were held between different people at the same time, which made the tape incoherent ... One advantage of actually interviewing one person while the group listens is that several individuals would not have otherwise said much, if they had to compete with some of the more verbally confident members.

Only in the first session did the tape seem to unnerve anyone. Once they had all heard some of the taping played back, and all laughed at each other's voices (in the main, mine!) it didn't seem to worry anyone.

What you actually tape is another whole area for debate. We ended up taping people's very personal experiences, and were very careful to localize the events by mentioning where they lived, where they saw the bombers, and so on, which consequently made it more interesting for the history students who lived in the same roads, and so on.

Near the end of the project, I arranged for some of the history

101

students, who were fourteen to fifteen years old, to join with the pensioners to hear and discuss the tapes that had been made. Various suggestions as to what else could be added or explained in further detail, were made, and were followed up at a later session.

This contact was extremely enjoyable and interesting, though quite strained at the start, due to shyness and ageist attitudes generally. Some of the students seemed totally shocked that the older women were approachable and interested in talking to them, and vice-versa. As this was so successful, various friendships were formed, with several of the students visiting the pensioners in their homes. This also led to Task Force being asked by the Social Science Department in the school to take a large part of their CSE course on "Ageism", as the students had found it so interesting. During this course, I invited several of the pensioners group into the lessons to help take them with me, which again was a huge success.

To spread the impact of the project and to pull in more information, the group compiled a questionnaire covering the same issues discussed on the tapes, which was then distributed to more housebound pensioners. A lot of this was done by groups of young Task Force volunteers from various local schools. This was particularly useful for it provided a starting point for conversation between the pupils and the old people, which led to friendships. It forged a link between the school and the local old people's home which has continued and led to various other activities, involving the older residents and the schoolchildren. In particular it has led onto discussions about the local school, as many of the people now in the home, had attended the school themselves seventy years ago.

Since the end of the project, the tapes have been used by various history departments in local schools, and listened to by several pensioners groups. Within Task Force, an organization with eleven centres accross London, it has promoted a lot of discussion, and ideas for similar projects in other London boroughs.'

Next, I want to look at the activities of a remarkable and resourceful group of elderly people in Bradford, The East Bowling History Workshop. They meet weekly to research and write the history of the East Bowling area of the city during the past century. This involves them in writing autobiographies and poetry, recording interviews, borrowing and copying old photographs, and publishing books. The story of their formation, their fund raising activities and their achievements, is told below, in the words of their secretary Evelyn Hanslip. This piece is taken from a talk given by the East Bowling History Workshop members at

Selby Community Centre in June 1981, in which they encouraged elderly people in Selby to form a similar group and write their own history.

East Bowling History Workshop started in September, 1978, when some people who had signed a paper in the local library, inviting anyone interested in forming a 'History Workshop', met in Fairfax School. Some wondered if they ought to have brought a bag of tools, but were reassured by Lydia Merril (Community Tutor) who said our object was to be the recording for publication of the history of East Bowling from about 1900, within our own lifetimes or those of our parents.

We had no money so some help would be needed. Bradford Central Library had published a booklet for a group writing about their 'Crown Comic Band', so we made an appointment and took a few stories we had written to show to a committee who run the Archives Dept. They said we should find a subject of universal interest, when they would consider the project.

We chose Bowling Tidings which for many years was held as Bradford Holiday Week, when all the mills closed down. We talked, borrowed old photographs, recorded memories from

Pasting up. The East Bowling History Workshop prepare a book for publication.

elderly local residents, and then began to write our stories out. These were criticised and pulled to pieces at meetings until they satisfied everyone. Then they were typed and photographs were chosen to illustrate them.

During this time we had two open meetings to which we invited any old pupils of our two largest local schools and this almost doubled our membership. We had an afternoon Summer Party which made us £10 profit, and we also applied to 'Yorkshire Arts Council' for a grant towards our work. This idea came from an advertisement in our local newspaper. The Yorkshire Arts Officer came to a meeting with two of his Committee and we eventually received a grant of £100. Now we had to open a Bank Account and form a Constitution.

We decided to try making a Calendar for fund raising, using six of our photographs of old Bowling scenes. Bradford College helped with typesetting and we put it together ourselves and sold them so quickly that we paid the Printers' bill out of the first profits.

Our first book *Bowling Tidings* arrived from the Metro Printers after a long delay and this sold out quickly and copies were sent to places all over the world. We have had one reprint which has also been sold out, and we are waiting for our second.

East Bowling Reflections was written in the same way, but was produced and paid for entirely by us and has been sold out once. We did a 1981 Calendar and received another £250 from 'Yorkshire Arts' last year. We were now also working at Bradford Mobile Workshop learning about the making up of books and the preparation of photography.

Our third book, *Gateway to Education*, about our early school life, is in its last stages and will soon be ready for typesetting.

We have had many enjoyable outings to interesting places, and quite a few speaking engagements, which we did not expect. Some universities have asked for our books and they are in our Bradford Libraries. 'Help the Aged' and 'Oral History Journal' have asked for our help, to our great surprise.

We hope that you will get started on recording the history of Selby and the surrounding villages as they were in the early part of the century. Your memories and reminiscences are too good to be lost in the inevitable changes that are taking place.

Reminiscence socials

One way of stimulating interest in oral history amongst the elderly, is to stage 'reminiscence socials' at local community centres, old people's homes, and so on. These should involve mobile displays of local history photographs and slides, combined with taped recollections and old documents and newspaper cuttings.

There might also be short dramatisations based on events in local history, or a 'Do You Remember?' quiz. The audience should be encouraged to take an active role, participating in discussions, contributing their own memories, and lending any relevant material they have for future displays. At the end of the 'social' you can invite those who are interested, to form or join a permanent oral history group. Task Force have had a great deal of success with Reminiscence Socials in London. For further information, contact Alan Bearne, 61c Coburg Street, London NW1 (enclosing a SAE).

Reminiscence aids

Some elderly people, for example the confused and the mentally handicapped, have lost the capacity and confidence to participate in a self-directed group. A Reminiscence Aid pack, containing autobiographies, photographs, slides, tapes, and so on, which focuses upon the recent history of the locality, can have a great therapeutic value when used with these people. Reminding them of their past can restore their personal dignity, give them a sense of perspective on life, and help them to cope with the present.

Oral history can provide elderly people with a new pride and purpose, which may at a later stage, enable them to play a more creative part in a project. Help The Aged have produced three Reminiscence Aid slide-tape packs for use with the elderly, called *Recall*. – Part 1, *Childhood and The Great War*, Part 2 *Youth and living through the Thirties*, and Part 3 *The Second World War: A Different World*. Each part comprises 40 slides and a cassette, and they cost £12 each. A recall handbook explaining how to use the material is available for around £3. For details contact, Help The Aged Education Department, 218 Upper St, London N1.

However, if you want a pack which relates specifically to your locality (and this is very important), you will probably have to make it yourself. Making such a pack can form the basis of an exciting project in itself.

17 Joining forces

If you want to organise an oral history group or project, you should think about joining forces with others working in your area. Getting together with others who have similar interests means you can exchange information, provide mutual support and share resources. There are four main groups active in oral history work – local history societies, History Workshop, The Oral History Society and The Federation of Worker Writers and Community Publishers. This second gives you information about them and their work, and the names and addresses of people to get in touch with.

Local history societies and classes

Until fairly recently most local historians restricted themselves to the use of documentary evidence, and concentrated on buildings and landscapes rather than the people who inhabited them. When people did come into focus they were usually local worthies – the mayor, the philanthropically minded manufacturer or the vicar – who would all be ritually slapped on the back for their good works.

However, in the past decade there has been a re-birth of local history, largely inspired by the new movements in social history that will be described a little later. People have now moved more towards the centre of the local history stage, and a number of societies are beginning to organise oral history projects and to publish valuable booklets and pamphlets.

There are several hundred local history societies in Britain – often at least a dozen in any one county – so if you are interested in joining there should be one fairly close to where you live. They usually arrange meetings about once a month, often attended by a couple of dozen people, arrange talks by local historians and organise outings and projects. A list of their names and addresses appears in *Local History Societies in England and Wales: A List* (1978) (see bibliography).

There is also a quarterly journal *The Local Historian* which contains advice, articles and information of interest both to professionals and part time enthusiasts working in this field. Many local history societies produce, either individually or collectively, occasional news-sheets and booklets. A short select list of some recent titles appears in the bibliography.

History Workshop

History Workshop is a loose coalition of full time socialist researchers and worker historians. It began in 1967 at Ruskin College, Oxford, when Raphael Samuel, together with his adult students drawn from the labour and trade union movement, sought to democratise the learning and writing of history in the college. To escape from the constraints of the exam system and conventional academic theory, they engaged in original historical research using primary source materials. This was a luxury usually reserved for post-graduate students. Their work, later published in a series of History Workshop pamphlets, was written from a Socialist perspective, and stressed the importance of the life experience of working class men and women in re-writing a more democratic history.

The enormous interest aroused by this radical approach, led to the organisation of annual history workshops, drawing hundreds of enthusiasts, which are still thriving today. A *History Workshop Journal*, published twice yearly, which acts as a focus for discussion, reports and research, was begun in 1975. The articles which appear in the journal and the main themes discussed at the annual conferences, reflect the Marxist, feminist and libertarian perspectives of those involved in the History Workshop movement. They often focus upon the experiences and struggles of oppressed groups such as the working class, women and children. Their work represents one of the most original and powerful contributions to radical and socialist history writing in the past decade.

The Oral History Society

The most active group which co-ordinates and communicates with the many people now interested in oral history, is the Oral History Society. It was formed in 1973 with the aim of encouraging the collection, preservation and publication of the tape recorded recollections of old people.

Most of those involved in oral history work see it as having enormous radical potential. In the words of Paul Thompson, a pioneer of the now flourishing oral history movement, 'It allows heroes not just from the leaders but from the unknown majority of the people. It provides a new basis for original projects, not just by professionals, but by students, by schoolchildren, or by the people of a community. They do not just have to learn their own history; they can write it. Oral history gives history back to the people in their own words. And in giving a past, it also helps them towards a future of their own making.'

The Society produces a twice-yearly journal, *Oral History*, edited by Paul Thompson and Joanna Bornat, which contains news and reports on work in Britain and abroad, practical and bibliographical advice, reviews, and a wide range of articles. It also stages two national meetings each year and assists in organising practical one day workshops for people wishing to start oral history projects. (For details see bibliography).

The Federation of Worker Writers and Community Publishers

The Federation was formed in 1976 when nine local groups active in this field decided to affiliate on a national level to exchange information and to provide mutual support. Since then the federation has steadily grown in strength and now embraces over twenty groups (see list on page 161).

One of the first initiatives in community publishing was taken in the early 1970's by Ken Worpole, an English teacher at Hackney Downs School in East London. He felt that most school books were irrelevant to the concerns of working class children. They simply could not identify with or interest themselves in mass produced, standardised reading material. To remedy this situation, he collaborated with local children to produce a book, 'The

108

Hackney Half Term Adventure', which focused upon their life experience, and sought to publish and distribute it in the locality. He persuaded the Centerprise bookshop in Hackney to publish it and it was received with immediate enthusiasm by local children and teachers, eventually selling several thousand copies. This and the follow up publications aroused enormous interest in the Hackney area, and local people who were writing autobiographies and poetry brought their work to Centerprise. In addition, local history classes were organised which provided further material for publications and exhibitions. The commitment of the Centerprise project to local people and local publishing has led to the successful production of around forty further titles.

There were parallel developments in other parts of the country, many of them born not out of an exclusive concern with recording and writing history, but rather out of local initiatives in community and political action. The Scotland Road Writer's Workshop for instance, was formed after a rent strike in a Liverpool dockside area. And Queen Spark Books grew out of a community campaign and a street newspaper in Brighton. All these groups were unified by a determination to resist elitism in all spheres of life, and to create a more democratic and libertarian local culture.

They aim to revitalise local working class culture by creating alternative centres for the production and distribution of books written essentially by and for local working class people. Most of their publications explore life experience through autobiography, local history based on oral interviews, photography, poetry and adult literacy material. They stage exhibitions, plays and readings at local venues as bookshops, community centres, libraries, pubs and schools. They also organise discussion groups, writer's workshops and local history classes, which are often radical in content and held in conjunction with the Worker's Educational Association.

One recent development in this field has been experimentation combining written pieces with poetry, songs and theatre in a radical 'cabaret' form. One of the pioneers in this field was 'Controlled Attack', a group spawned by the Stepney Basement Writers, comprising three local young working class people who performed a political, new wave cabaret for several years. They took their show to many community centres and schools in London's East End, performed on the 'new variety' London cabaret circuit in pubs and clubs and made a tour of the North of England. For details of how to join the FWWCP and a guide to the work they have produced, see bibliography.

To give you the flavour of the life histories that have been produced by the FWWCP. I want to finish this section with some extracts taken from two autobiographies.

In *The Town Beehive: A Young Girl's Lot, Brighton 1910–1934*, published by Queen Spark Books (60p), Daisy Noakes vividly describes her working class upbringing and her young days in service. In the extract below, she tells how a sexist convention and her own innocence led to the loss of her first love.

> I got very friendly with one boy named Jess. He was an only child and seemed quieter and more sensible than the others. I singled him out to walk with, on returning from my half day, and when I had an hour off in the evening I knew he would be round about his father's stable. I would help clean his horse brasses, and I grew quite fond of him.
>
> When I was leaving him one evening, he put his arm round my shoulders and gave me a kiss. I shall never forget the feeling I had. I could never explain it, but it was the first sign of affection I had ever had, and I was walking on air. I was sure this was real love, and became more friendly by asking him to come home to tea with me.
>
> I was sitting astride the bottom half of the stable door one Sunday morning, when Mrs M. went by on her way to Church. She gave me a scathing glance and passed on. I was summoned to the study on her return, to be told that when I was off duty on Sunday mornings I was to go to Church, and not flirt with village boys.
>
> My friendship with Jess came to a sudden end. I knew his birthday was near, so I bought a pair of military hair brushes in a case, and had a silver J put on the backs. I knocked at his cottage door. No one came, but his mother popped her head out of an upstair window to inquire what I wanted. I told her I had brought Jess's birthday present. She accused me of running after him, told me to stay away. If he wanted me – he would come to me.
>
> My heart sank into my boots. I could not see at the time that I was over-doing things. I went away and cried and cried. In fact, I cried off and on for days. Something had happened to Jess. He avoided me. So that was the end of Love's Young Dream.

In *Toby*, published by Bristol Broadsides (65p) we hear the voice of a remarkable tramp who went on the road, sleeping rough, while a young man during the Depression years in the 1930s. He

Daisy Noakes working as a domestic servant at Ovingdean Hall, near Brighton, in 1924.

enjoyed the closeness to nature, the solitude and the time to reflect so much, that he continued tramping for the next forty years. In the following extract he recalls an incident that occured in the 1930s after he moved on from a London hostel to avoid police harassment.

I got outside and I said to this cockney chap, 'Excuse me mate, which road out for Edmonton?' That's north London. 'Edmonton?' he said. 'You can get a so and so number bus'. I said, 'I'm not interested in the bus, I'm walking'. He nearly fell down. He said, 'What! Walking?' I said, 'Sure, I've got all day, twelve miles, that's nothing'.

111

Toby the Tramp.

So I ambled on. I arrived at tea time at Scarface's. They called it Scarface's because the porter there was attacked one time and had a very bad scar. Scarface's was a spike. I was a bit tired like. It was hot weather, in the summer. I was terribly fatigued walking through London in the hustle and bustle. When I got there, what do I find? A queue of us waiting to be booked in and there's these chapel women there issuing tracts to the poor tramps. A woman comes to me with a tract. I said, 'I'm not interested in them'.

'Why aren't you?' she said. 'Look lady!' I said 'I've come a days march today. I'm tired. All I'm thinking of now is getting something to eat in there, and a bath and then to bed. The trouble with you people is your approach. You've got the wrong technique, you do it wrong. If you want to get a man to listen, if he's on the road, first ask him if he's hungry. If he says, "Yes, I could do with a meal", take him, feed him and when he's satisfied with his physical needs, he'll listen to you and your spiritual needs'. I don't know if I left a mark on her. I know what it is to be really hungry, friendless, cold, wet, slept rough, all of it.

I never got depressed on the road. I get more depressed sometimes thinking about the state of the world to be truthful. Its a sad, sick world. I've got a feeling about it, it could be different. You could throw out all the greed and malice and selfishness, hatred and things like that. I can dispell it out of my mind. I'm like a child.

There is hope, but as the world is now you've got separate governments, national barriers, prejudice and you've got industrial powers. As long as you've got that you'll never get peace in the world when mankind could walk in dignity and with humility. That's the way I see it.

When you're a tramp you're ostracised by people and they condemn you, I had all that but it doesn't worry me. If you meet only one good person it makes up for all the bad ones.

One woman looked at me. She said, 'Why do you live a life like that?' The way she emphasised it with disdain, I could tell that she was against it. Well I said, 'Its like this lady. I've decided to emancipate from the social vortex, from life's perplexities to the tranquilities of nature'. Her eyes were popping out of her head. She didn't say no more.

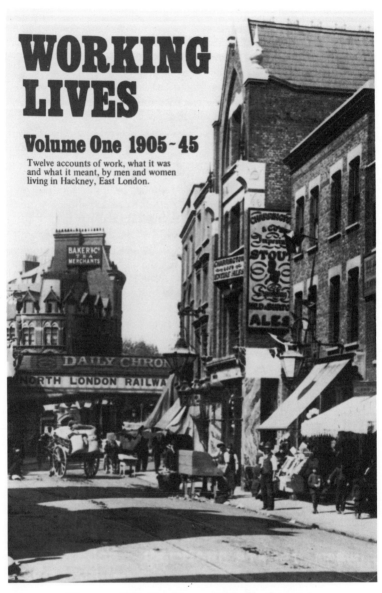

The cover of *Working Lives, published by Centerprise*

Part four:
How to present,
publish and preserve
your material

18 Presentation design, and printing

One of the prime aims of the oral history movement is to put people into print, especially people who would normally be denied this opportunity. This fourth part of the book is a step-by-step guide to how to present, design, print, market and finance, whatever you want to publish. It could be a leaflet, a pamphlet or a book – the main principles are the same.

Writing – some advice on presentation

There should always be critical discussion about the writing that emerges from oral history projects. Everything produced, whether autobiography, local history, corrected transcripts of tapes, and so on, should be examined by the whole group. Only in this way can we develop our ideas and our ability to communicate through the written word. I want here to offer some advice on presentation. The craft of writing cannot be chiselled down into a few paragraphs. But there are two basic tools of the trade that need to be explained to those about to embark on a publishing project. These are, clarity and good titles. They will help you to fashion your material into a shape which is more accessible and appealing to your audience.

Some do's and don'ts of clear writing

Do organise your material in an orderly way so that it 'adds up'. The two most common ways of organising oral history material are to put it in a chronological form or use a particular theme.

Do use a style that is appropriate for the audience you are aiming at.

117

Do use fairly short sentences. Long sentences are often difficult to understand. Short sentences are clear and powerful.

Do use short paragraphs. It makes the text more appetising for the reader.

Do use the same word twice or even three times in the same sentence if it makes your idea clearer.

Don't express more than one idea in one sentence.

Don't take too much knowledge for granted on the part of the reader.

Don't use cliches and over used expressions such as, 'Rule the roost' and 'thin end of the wedge', phrases like these are as tired out as fashionable media words like scenario, syndrome and credibility.

Some suggestions for good titles

A powerful and intriguing title attracts attention, makes a good book better and helps to sell it. It should capture not only the main theme of the book, but also the imagination of the reader. How do you conjure up such a title? Here are some basic rules.

1. Personalise it. Personal experience has power and authenticity. It rings true and is what oral history is all about. Some examples are – *In My young Days*, *When I was a Child*, *Arthur and Me* and *Bristol as We Remember it*.

2. Use local place names to attract local interest and sell most of your copies locally. Some examples are, *Stepney Words*, *A Hoxton Childhood* and *Up Knowle West*.

3. Alliteration, the repetition of the initial sound in successive words can make your title sing. Two examples are, *Coronation Cups and Jam Jars* and *A Licence to Live*.

4. Use a phrase taken from the book to encapsulate what the book is all about. Some examples are, *The World in a Classroom* and *The Voice of the Past* and *For Gawdsake Don't Take Me*.

5. Give cliches and proverbs a twist to give them a new lease of life and to fix the reader's attention. Some examples are, *Rebels With a Cause*, *The Good Old Bad Old Days* and *The Gender Trap*.

6. Be controversial. If your book is taking issue with something or somebody, don't keep it a secret but shout it out loud! Some examples are, *Classrooms of Resistance, Teaching as a Subversive Activity* and *The Female Eunuch*.

7. Use sub-titles where necessary. A catchy title often needs to be complemented by a sub-title which clarifies the content of the book. For example, *The Gender Trap: A Closer Look at Sex Roles*.

Design

If you want your pamphlet or book to make an impact on the reader you must design it in an eye catching and attractive way. There are three main elements in the design process to think about.

The text

Moving your eyes across page after page of unrelieved typing has a similar effect to long distance motorway driving. It numbs the brain. You need signposts all the way through the text to give the readers a clear idea of what direction they're moving in, to help them find what they are looking for, and to show them the beginning and end of each section. You also need the signposts of chapter divisions and headings in most books.

Also try to arrange the text in fairly short paragraphs. Leave at least ½ inch margins on both sides of the page and keep the margin consistent throughout. Don't be afraid to leave spaces between different sections – they help to break up the monotony of the print. Use a reasonably large type size and a carbon ribbon on your typewriter for a clearer printed image.

The illustrations

Illustrations increase the interest and impact of what you are saying, and can leave a vivid impression in the reader's mind. There are two types of illustration (or 'artwork'), drawings and photographs. By using a pen and ink, biro or felt tip, you can draw cartoons, diagrams, maps and sketches onto your 'master' copy or stencil.

Photographs are slightly more complicated. They have to be

converted mechanically into a black and white dotted image by a process called 'screening'. If you want to try your hand at this, a full explanation is given in Jonathan Zeitlyn, *Print: How You Can Do It Yourself*, Inter-Action Inprint (1980). If not, most commercial printers and some community presses provide this service.

On pages where you are using drawings and photos, you should plan the best possible layout by making a 'mock up'. This is just a simple sketch of the positioning of each illustration which gives you a chance to play around with various possibilities before actually committing yourself to print.

The final stage is to gum the items down onto the 'master' sheet, a thin sheet of card of the appropriate size. Rule in a grid system in blue pencil on it (this is a series of margins at least ½ inch wide at the top, bottom and sides of your page) which helps you to stick the drawings and photographs down at right angles and in the right places. You can lay out your page any size you want if you are using offset litho printing, as it can be reduced or enlarged photographically for printing.

Spread a thin layer of glue on the card and on the back of the illustration. The best glue to use is Cow Gum which doesn't dry for several minutes and you can move items around if you make mistakes. It is important to keep your artwork as clean as possible, otherwise smudges will spoil the final product. Paint out any dirty marks with white correcting fluid and rub out dry, excess Cow Gum using a Cow Gum rubber. You can make one of these by rolling together a ball of dry Cow Gum.

The cover

The cover is the first thing that potential readers see. If it grabs their attention they will leaf through the pages, but if not, the book remains untouched on the shelf. The most basic way to produce an appealing front cover is to use a coloured card as a base. White covers quickly become shop-soiled. Then gum onto it and letraset the title and author's name in bold print in the top and bottom margins. You can get lots of other ideas by browsing around bookshops.

Use the back cover for a short blurb describing the book, mentioning your group and possibly listing some of your other publications. Stapling is the cheapest and most common method used by community publishers to fasten together booklets.

120

Printing

Four of the most common forms of do-it-yourself printing are photocopying, spirit duplicating, stencil duplicating and offset litho printing. If you need more details about these and other printing methods, you should read Jonathan Zeitlyn's book, *Print: How You Can Do It Yourself*, Inter-Action Inprint (1980).

Advantages and disadvantages of printing by different methods.

The cost section gives the approximate price of printing 500 A4 copies using four different methods:

Photocopying

Advantages: accessibility, speed and simplicity.
Disadvantages: expensive for large quantities.
Cost: at 5p a shot, total £25
      at 10p a shot, total £50

Spirit duplicator

Advantages: fairly cheap and simple.
Disadvantages: quality of reproduction not very sharp.
Cost: 5 stencils 30 p, 1 Ream (500 sheets) £2.50, total = £2.80.

Stencil duplicating

Advantages: fairly cheap and simple.
Disadvantages. Ink sometimes seeps through onto print offs.
Cost. 2 stencils 30p, 1 Ream £2.50, total = £2.80.

Offset litho printing

Advantages: cheap for large quantities and better quality reproductions than any of the above methods.
Disadvantages: These machines are not widely available in resource centres and are more complicated to operate.
Cost: 500 copies of same sheet printed on both sides (approx.) £7–15. 1,000 copies of same sheet printed on both sides (approx.) £10–18.
It gets cheaper the more you print. Prices vary according to whether you have photographs which cost more.

19 Marketing

To a community publishing project operating on a shoestring budget, high or low sales often means the difference between financial solvency and bankruptcy so you should always think long and hard about how to market a publication effectively before you start. Unless you have substantial reserves of capital you should only publish booklets that you are reasonably confident will sell enough copies to pay for themselves. Aim to break even or there is a good chance that your publishing project will suddenly sink without trace. This section will give you some general advice on how to avoid such disasters, and how to sell your publications to a wide readership. For a community publisher there are three main processes involved in marketing; costing, fund raising and publicity and sales.

Costing

You will have to make decisions about the price of the publication and how many copies to print.

When you fix the price of your publication you must include all your costs in your calculations. One common mistake made by people new to publishing is to underprice their books. This usually happens because people assume that manufacturing costs are the only major costs likely to be incurred (remember that in commercial publishing the list price is usually around five to six times the direct cost of manufacture). Of course a community publishing project, using mainly voluntary labour, can reduce or cut out some of the costs incurred by commercial publishers, and there are no profit margins to push prices up.

But you are still likely to incur many expenses over and above typesetting, printing and binding costs. If you sell through high street bookshops they will tend to keep around 35 per cent of the cover price. On top of this you have to allow for unsold stock, interest rates, publicity, editorial overheads, and photographic and screening costs. All these costs must be reflected and recovered in the price you charge. To give you a clearer idea of how to balance total expenditure with total expected earnings, a typical community publication budget is given below.

The decision on how many copies to print, (the 'print run') requires careful consideration. The cost per copy will reduce if you increase the run but never print more than you expect to sell in eighteen months because tying up your money in stock is expensive and risky. The print runs used by community publishers usually vary between 1,000 and 3,000 copies so, as a general rule, if you are a new group launching your first publication, don't print more than 1,000 copies.

When you have decided on your print run, obtain two or three quotes from different printers. The main consideration in choosing a printer is cheapness. But other factors to take into

---

PUBLICATION BUDGET

1,500 copies of a 96 page, illustrated A5 book, plus cover, selling at £1.45.

Costs

Photographic and screening costs......................	50
Typesetting, printing and binding costs...............	1300
35 per cent discount to booksellers on third of stock (over two thirds sold direct)......................	200
15 per cent discount for distribution on third of stock	90
Publicity, promotion and review copies................	70
Allowance for unsold stock............................	200
Allowance for bad debts and invoicing costs...........	80
Editorial overheads (travel, telephone, stationery etc)	40
TOTAL COSTS	**£2030**

Income

Sale of 1500 copies @ £1.45 each......................	1875
Total trust fund aid..................................	155
	£2030

account are reliability, speed, quality and the period of credit offered if any.

For books or pamphlets printers will tend to use large sheets made up of 8, 16 or 32 pages on their presses. So try to ensure that the length of your publication is in multiples of 8, 16 or 32 pages, otherwise you will be paying for a lot of waste paper. A large local firm with in-house printing could be persuaded to let you use their machinery free, or there might be a community resource centre nearby which offers cheap printing to community projects.

Finance

How do you raise the initial capital needed to pay for the printing costs of a pamphlet or book? Borrowing from the bank, pooling the resources of your collective and trying to obtain credit from the printers should give you some breathing space and cover most of the initial costs. But there are other sources of financial aid:

1. The local council. Find out which is the appropriate committee before making a written application as it could be either the arts, recreation, leisure, or social services committee. You could also check for funding under the Urban Aid Scheme.

2. Foundations, another name for a grant-making trust, number several thousand in Britain. They will usually only support particular causes, for example child welfare, education or scientific research, so before making an application check that they have a particular interest in your area and type of work. Look at *The Directory of Grant Making Trusts* which is available in most libraries, and gives detailed information on foundations and the amount of money they have available.

3. Regional Arts Associations. For details see Michael Norton, *The Directory of Social Change Vol. 2 Community* (1977) p. 83.

4. Local fund giving groups, like the Round Table or Rotary Club or trade unions, can occasionally be persuaded to contribute small sums, especially if your project has particular relevance to them.

5. Local firms can sometimes be persuaded to make donations of equipment or money but they may try to influence the project so you should be aware of this.

6. Fund raising events such as benefit performances, raffles, jumble sales, sponsored walks, and so on can be very time-consuming but they do help to involve a lot of people in your project even if the financial return is small.

How to write a fund raising proposal

Applying for financial aid has become more difficult with the recent cutbacks in state funding and the economic recession. You will do well to rustle up two or three hundred pounds in this way. Your success will depend to a large extent on the quality of the fund raising proposal that you write. Advice on how to compose a letter of proposal is contained in *The Directory of Social Change Vol. 2 Community* p. 205–209.

Registering as a charity

Once you begin publishing non profit-making pamphlets and books, you should seriously consider seeking charitable status for your group or project. Charities enjoy many financial advantages, particularly in terms of tax and rate relief. Your group would probably qualify for charitable status under the category 'advancement of education' or 'other purposes beneficial to the community'. For a guide on charitable status, its benefits, and how to get it, see Andrew Phillips and Keith Smith, *Charitable Status: A Practical Handbook*, Inter-Action Inprint (1980).

Publicity and sales

A well planned and well timed publicity campaign is essential if you are to sell your book to your target readership. A community publishing group with limited funds for a campaign should combine minimum costs with the promise of maximum sales returns. There are several different elements in such a campaign, the most important of which is organising an extensive local sales network, and a local media launch to coincide with the date of publication.

Local distribution

One of the main aims of the oral history movement is to enable local people to share and study their life experiences together.

Thus it is very important to sell most of your publications locally, because local people are most likely to find them particularly interesting and relevant. There are two main methods of achieving intensive local sales.

First, through personal contacts. The members of your collective must each carry books around and sell them at local clubs, pubs, community events, meetings, readings and from door to door. The collective should also telephone or write to local schools, adult education groups, community centres, libraries, museums and political organisations, to encourage them to become involved in your project and buy copies of your books. Further interest can be stimulated if you produce posters. A4 size is best because it won't use up too much precious wall space and you can usually run off 100 A4 posters at a community silk screen shop for about £15. You can display them in libraries, schools, shops, and so on or if you have your own alternative/community bookshop you can use this as a base and sell many copies of your books through it.

The advantage of face to face contact is that it develops

An adult literacy group at work on the 'Milk River' publishing project in South London.

personal relationships between authors, the members of the collective and the local readership. This is a feature often missing from the depersonalised relationships found in commercial publishing. By selling direct you can hold down the price of your books simply because you by-pass the middlemen used by commercial publishers who are anxious to make profits. For these reasons, some community publishing groups like Queen Spark in Brighton, refuse to sell through the high street or 'straight' bookshops, and achieve local sales of several thousand by face to face contacts alone.

The second method you can use is the more conventional one of selling through local bookshops and newsagents. This will push your sales up, but it will also push your prices up because the shops will probably demand 35 per cent of the cover price for themselves. However, if you don't have your own bookshop or a wide network of local contacts, you will probably have to sell some of your books in this way, at least to begin with.

Local media coverage

It should be fairly easy to get a feature on your book in the local press and on local radio and television. Try to arrange for this publicity to coincide with the first day or week of publication. Press features usually have the most impact. Send a one or two page press release to your local newspapers describing the book in short, punchy sentences and offer review copies. Remember that many journalists will quote verbatim from it, so give them a few juicy extracts and some direct speech to lift. Also, inform them whether or not the author is available for interview. This is particularly important when negotiating for radio and television coverage. You can cut costs by sending the same press release to them. Prepare your author for media interviews by having a few 'dummy runs' with them. In fact you can often tell the producer the questions you want your author to be asked. Remember to ensure that the title of your book gets a mention at the beginning or the end of the interview. All these matters are explained in more detail in a very useful book, *Using The Media: How to Deal with the Press, Television and Radio* by Denis Macshane (Pluto 1979).

Other methods of boosting sales

Entries in bibliographies and bookseller's journals are one of the cheapest ways of promoting a publication and selling it to

127

libraries and bookshops. To do this you send a free copy to Whitaker's Book List Editor and to the main copyright libraries. For addresses and further advice, see Keith Smith, *Marketing For Small Publishers*, Inter-Action Inprint (1980).

Journal reviews act like a free advertisement for your publication. Send free review copies to any journal or magazine that might find your title of interest. Address them to the 'Review Editor', and in each one enclose a review slip giving details of the title, author, price and publication date, and requesting a copy of the review. You can find details of all the journals that are currently published listed under subject headings in *Willings Press Guide* (East Grinstead – updated each year) and *Ulrich's International Periodicals Directory* (New York 1980).

Postal publicity involves offering people your publications by post. Because postage is becoming increasingly expensive it is advisable to use postal publicity only when it is free or almost free. Insert a publicity sheet in your regular mailing to members (if you

Looking through the local history publications at the Centerprise bookshop in Hackney.

have any) or any free enclosures in the mailings of fraternal organisations.

Alternative bookshops are very important in boosting sales. There are three ways that you can reach them with your publications. First, you can write to them direct. Secondly, you can negotiate a deal with the Publications Distribution Co-operative (PDC), which distributes community publications to bookshops, especially community bookshops, all over the country. Thirdly, you can affiliate to the Federation of Worker Writers and Community Publishers. Many of these local groups revolve around alternative bookshops and they make arrangements to sell each other's titles in their shops. Further information on how to use these outlets is contained in Keith Smith's *Marketing For Small Publishers op. cit.* This book also maps out a clear path if you want to venture into the highly capitalised jungle of commercial bookshops.

Library sales. If you are publishing titles of local interest it is worth circulating all the branch libraries in your area. They can often be persuaded to take at least one copy. Most of your other library sales will spring from the interest aroused by the entries in bibliographies and journal reviews that you have arranged.

20 Local Radio

The unrealised potential of Local Radio

Oral history has enormous potential for broadcasting on local radio. It has the potential to stimulate a high level of interest and identification amongst local people. But this potential has rarely been realised. Few radio stations have regular local radio features or programmes, and few community groups have attempted to participate in the making of such programmes.

In the past two decades there has been an increase in the number of BBC local radio and independent commercial stations. Many major cities now have local radio. This gives a local oral history group or project a golden opportunity to reach a wide audience. Further, you can encourage the participation of local people in making these programmes.

Most local radio stations will take any proposals you have for an oral history project on the air very seriously. This is for two reasons. First, they are eager to develop a closer relationship with the listeners and the localities that they serve. Secondly, they are often under-financed, and have little money to spend on promotion and programming. As a result they are often keen for contributions to existing programmes and will listen to ideas for new series.

Your group will be most likely to succeed in getting a local radio spot or series, if you can convince the controllers that you are capable of making programmes which are of comparable production and sound quality to those made by the professionals. Although there is a mystique which surrounds the world of broadcasting, most of the skills and techniques used by media professionals are fairly straightforward and simple to understand. This section will explain all you need to know to make your own radio feature, programme or series.

What type of programme?

The two types of local radio programme your group can aim to produce or participate in are 'open access' and 'structured access' programmes.

Open access programmes are those in which people outside the professional staff, are given the opportunity to use the recording and broadcasting facilities of the station and more important, they have complete editorial control over what is broadcast. The only limit is the law of libel. Access broadcasting gives you the chance to shed new light on subjects which may have been overlooked or misrepresented by the established media.

In fact, few open access local radio programmes of this type are broadcast. But the BBC and the IBA (the controlling body for independent local radio) have accepted a commitment to providing opportunities for this type of programme as part of their public service obligations. So if your local station controllers reject your proposals out of hand, remind them of this commitment.

In structured access programmes much more editorial control is maintained by the professional programme producer at the station. If you see eye-to-eye with the producer on the theme of your programme, the problem of control will rarely arise. But if there is a conflict of interest or opinion, the producer will invariably win, and you may well find your material either censored or not presented in the manner you would wish.

There are two main forms of structured access programme which you should aim for: magazine programmes and local history programmes.

Magazine programmes usually consist of popular music interspersed with chat, news, phone-ins, quizzes, occasional interviews, information about entertainments and exhibitions, and features on leisure activities such as gardening, sport and cookery.

Producers will usually be keen to vary the content with an occasional or regular oral history feature if you prepare the material for them.

Some radio stations broadcast local history programmes. If your local station does, you should consider collaborating with the producer and feeding in your ideas and material. Although there is less experimentation in this area than there might be, there are

The oral history project at Whitefield School was featured on Radio Bristol's 'Six O' Clock Rock Show'.

some pioneering producers around, with whom you might be able to develop a fruitful relationship. For example, in the 1970s, Arthur Wood of Radio Stoke-on-Trent and Dennis Stuart of Keele University's Adult Education Department, conceived a project on local social history with the aim of encouraging listeners to contribute to and participate in radio programmes. They organised local study groups and the material they produced formed the basis of a series of programmes composed of interview extracts, dramatisations and narration. As a result, many people began writing about their life experiences and offered to be interviewed. The series ran for eighty weeks.

Getting on the air

How do you go about getting your group and the recordings you have made, on the air? There are four main stages:

1. Locate your nearest local radio station. A list appears in the *Writers and Artists Yearbook* (Adam and Charles Black), which is

updated each year and available at most libraries (see also *Using the Media* op cit). In most areas it will be either a BBC station or a commercial IBA station. But in some big cities you will find both. If there is a choice it is worth remembering that commercial stations tend to have a bias towards a younger audience so to get airtime for an oral history project on commercial radio, you should have young people involved either as interviewers or organisers.

2. Type out a letter, sketching out your programme ideas, and send it to your local station. Explain who you and your organisation are, and briefly describe the length, subject matter and audience that you have in mind for your proposed programmes. Offer to make a 'pilot' feature; a one-off experimental spot. Suggest a meeting with the producer to discuss the idea further. Address the letter to the 'Open Access Producer' as there is usually one producer at each station with specific responsibility for open access programming.

Producers are always open to offers of features but remember that outside contributors (apart from the regular freelance staff) are rarely paid, not even their expenses. So it's best not to spoil your chances at this early stage by demanding a fat cheque; offer a *free* feature.

3. Make sure that your feature contains some extracts which whet the appetite of the producer for more. If possible, use a Uher machine for your recordings. The sound quality of your extracts will then match up to the high standards that professional broadcasters set.

4. Produce a more detailed synopsis or outline of the content of each feature or programme, and discuss it with the producer.

To complete Stages 3 and 4 successfully you will need some technical knowledge of what makes good radio and how and what to edit. These will each be dealt with in turn.

Four rules of good radio

There are a number of different ways of organising and presenting oral history material for a radio feature or programme and you should choose the form of presentation which best suits the material you have to hand. There is the single life history, a collection of life histories, or a cross analysis of them.

Whichever form you choose to use, there are four basic rules of good radio that you should follow when making your programme.

1. Ensure that it is clearly structured. This is essential to a radio programme of this type. Without it the material becomes confusing and incomprehensible to the listener. It must all add up and lead the listener somewhere. There are two main elements that make a sound structure.

First, the basic framework. Every oral history programme should have a beginning, a middle and an end. The beginning and the end are the most important. If your beginning is powerful, the listener is likely to stay tuned into your programme. If your ending is memorable, the listener will probably reflect on what he/she has heard and listen to the next one if the programme is part of a series. So, you should always try to arrange it so that you are using some of your most moving extracts and are making some of your most powerful points, at the beginning and at the end of each programme.

The second essential element an oral history programme must have, is a clear argument or theme that is followed throughout. Don't make it too general. A programme that attempts to cover a subject like 'Life in the 1930s', will probably be swamped by the wealth of material available. Try to make your theme more specific than this. For example you might decide upon; 'growing up', 'poverty' or 'unemployment in the 1930s'. Once you have a manageable theme try to arrange the extracts so that they state an argument. For example, if you were making a programme on 'growing up in the 1930s', you might decide to select extracts on rebellion against authority and try to arrange the material so that it attempts to answer important questions like; 'Why did this rebellion occur?'

2. The relevance of the material to the theme is a very important principle to keep in mind. When editing your material you should ask yourself, 'What can I leave out?', rather than 'What can I leave in because I am short of material?' Often, you have to be ruthless to keep a programme tight and to the point. When you have completed it, you should be able to honestly say that it is not possible to lose a single sentence from the programme, because every one is relevant.

134

If a speaker pauses for a long time, wanders off the point or tells a story that is irrelevant to your main theme, cut it. Make sure that you don't unintentionally repeat exactly the same point several times in the mouths of different speakers. You don't have much time to play with on a radio broadcast, so make the most of it.

3. Variety between different extracts helps to sustain the interest of the listener. If you are using different voices, you could consider arranging them so that a short extract is followed by a long extract, a man's voice is followed by a woman's or a person who speaks quickly is followed by one who speaks slowly. Different accents also offer scope for creating contrast within a programme, if they are directly juxtaposed.

In addition, you might consider using appropriate sound effects or music, either in the background or as a bridge between different extracts. A well chosen sound – perhaps a traditional work song, the ringing of an old school bell, or the clump of horse's hooves on cobbled streets – can vividly recapture life as it

Arran school children interviewing in the classroom – fascinating local radio programmes can be made out of life stories.

135

was lived in a previous era. The BBC produce an excellent series of sound effects records which can be used.

You might also consider using a speaker to read an extract from contemporary, documentary source material – perhaps a press report, a social investigation, a school log book, and so on – to add another dimension to the memories you are using.

The above points should not be adopted slavishly. There will be occasions when narrated extracts and sound effects will dam the natural flow of a programme, and divert the listener's attention away from its main theme. But if used with care, these techniques can help you to paint a sound picture, with contrasting strokes of light and shade, which holds the interest and imagination of the listener.

4. There should be a natural flow throughout the programme. Voices and sounds should be combined so that they make a unified and authentic whole.

Natural flow is particularly important if you decide to use little or no formal narration by a presenter, and everything unfolds through the mouths of the people interviewed. This is called the 'stream of consciousness' technique. Many producers of life history programmes use this type of presentation, because natural speech is much more compelling than scripted speech. However, it is often much more time consuming and difficult to construct a programme in this way. For it to work, the extracts must be self explanatory, and they must be arranged in a logical and thematic progression which is easily understandable.

The interviewer's questions and responses often distract the listener's attention. They should be cut out whenever possible. Try to create the impression that the speaker is talking directly to the listener.

When you are editing tapes, a few minor difficulties sometimes arise which threaten to impair the natural flow of the speech. As long as you plan carefully which extract is to follow which, with the continuity and harmony of the speech in mind, these problems can usually be avoided. Always ensure that the voice inflection at the end of one piece, is compatible with the voice inflection of the spliced piece. In some circumstances it may be necessary to insert an inch or two of blank 'leader' tape, in order to provide a pause, thereby making the join sound more natural. Another difficulty sometimes arises when there is a background noise on the actual recording, for example the slow ticking of a grandfather clock. Beware of cutting sections like these – the join is likely to be audible to the listener. Sometimes minor discrepancies can be compensated for by laying further effects of a similar type over the top.

What to edit – an example

By now you will have realised that making a radio programme involves a lot of editing. To give you a clearer idea of how you go about constructing an extract with natural flow out of a series of questions and answers, I want to use, as an example, part of an interview with an old Bristolian lady called Ada Iles, which I used for a BBC radio broadcast. This particular extract lasted, in all, for just ninety seconds, but it was edited down from a ninety minute interview.

This single extract was constructed out of four separate parts taken from different moments in the interview. The order that she originally told the stories in was reversed to make them clearer and flow more naturally from one to the other. This is an acceptable practice when editing a radio programme, as long as you are careful not to distort the meaning of what is said.

The italics indicate words and sections that were edited out of the original interview. The bold type indicates what was left in to make the extract that was broadcast:

Mind, I used to be a proper tomboy and harum scarum.
Interviewer. *Did you?*
Yes. What the boys did do, I could do.
Interviewer. *Did you used to fight them in the streets?*
Fight with 'em, yes. I'd do anything the boys did do.
Interviewer. *Did you win?*
No, not very often. Might have a couple of clouts or punches.
(Ada continues her description of fighting, but she doesn't tell any anecdotes that are long enough to use.)
(Insert the following quote taken from the beginning of the interview.) *But* **we used to climb walls, crawl through hedges. I can remember once, we was caught, the man what made us, caught us, and the man made us eat some sour apples. He said 'now you've picked 'em, now you eat 'em.**
(Ada continues her description of the pranks she played. None of them are told clearly enough to be broadcast.)

137

(Insert the following quote taken from further on in the interview.)
We had a big quarry up by us, and we used to go up there with the boys, sliding down the quarry on old tins. Well, I used to come home with me pants broke, and my sister did sew 'em up for me so that our mam shouldn't know.
(Ada continues her description of the games she played. Again they are too short and disjointed to be broadcast.)
(Insert the following quote taken from towards the end of the interview.)
We used to climb up the lamposts, because it was gas lamposts then, you know, gas like, and we used to climb up and break the mantles. 'Course, we didn't think the gas was still escaping, we didn't realise that. Too ignorant. But we used to do it and run away. Well, the police would go after us, if they had any ideal of that, because it was dangerous.
Interviewer. *Would they hit you if they caught you?*
They'd clout your ears, the coppers. Kick the boys up the backside. Whereas now, if they catch 'em they summons 'em, in they days, if they caught 'em doing anything like that, they'd kick 'em up the backside.

How to edit

There are two main stages in tape editing. First, re-recording the relevant sections of the original tape onto another known as 'dubbing'. Secondly, physically cutting the recorded material, known as 'cutting and splicing'.

To dub from one tape to another you need two recorders. Plug them into each other using an appropriate extension lead supplied by the manufacturer. Select the extracts you want to re-record for your programme, then press the play button down on the machine containing the original tape. Simultaneously press the play and record buttons down on the machine containing the copy tape.

In this way you will be able to rough edit an original tape down to manageable proportions. When rough editing always leave several seconds of speech either side of each extract that you intend to use. If you do this you won't run the risk of cutting into and spoiling the beginning and the end of each extract when you start to edit the material.

This is a useful technique because it enables you to avoid cutting the original tape and to preserve it in its entirety for an

138

Cutting tapes in preparation for a broadcast on Radio Bristol.

archive. For a radio programme you will often only need to use two or three minutes highlights out of an original interview lasting for perhaps two or three hours.

The next stage is to smooth out the rough edges – eliminating digressions, interviewer's questions, long pauses, unwanted sounds, and so on – by cutting and splicing the tape. This process is very easy and can be divided up into ten parts.

1. You need the following tools for the job. An editing block (sometimes known as a tape splicer), leader tape, splicing tape, a spare tape spool, and a chinagraph pencil. All these items can be bought either separately or as a complete tape editing kit at most audio shops. The total cost should be under £5. You will also need a pair of scissors.

2. Stop the tape just before the unwanted speech making sure that you are not too close to any speech that you want to keep. Mark the section of tape which has just emerged from the playback head on the right of the recorder with the chinagraph pencil.

3. Remove the tape from the recorder by lifting up each spool simultaneously. Place the left hand spool to the left of the editing

block, and the right hand spool to the right. If the tape becomes twisted, straighten it out by turning one of the spools a full circle.

4. Place the section of tape to be cut along the groove in the editing block, shiny side down. These grooves are designed to take the exact width of the tape, thus ensuring that the tapes are perfectly straight when they are cut and joined together.

5. Line up the precise point on the tape marked by the chinagraph pencil, so that it lies directly underneath the blade on the editing block. When you get it in the correct position press the clamps down on either side of the blade. These hold the tape firmly while the splicing is being carried out. Then press the blade down onto the tape. This is usually operated by a spring mechanism.

6. Lift up the right hand clamp and remove the right hand tape. Place a section of leader tape, shiny side facing down, from right to left in the groove, slightly overlapping the diagonal cut on the original tape. Secure the leader tape by bringing down the right hand clamp. Then press the blade down. The original tape and the leader tape will then meet diagonally in a smooth join. The blade on an editing block always makes a diagonal cut because this type of join doesn't make any noise when it passes over the tape head.

7. Cut off a section of splicing tape about one inch long, then press it down onto the join overlapping the cut by about half an inch on each side. Ensure that the splicing tape does not overlap the width of the recording tape even by a fraction of an inch. Otherwise it will become jammed inside the machine.

8. Remove the clamps and cut off around six inches of leader tape. Then attach the end to an empty spool having first placed the left hand spool in position on the machine.

9. Play the tape forward and stop it at the end of the unwanted speech. Mark the tape on the right hand side of the tape head with the chinagraph pencil. Then repeat procedures 2–5 and dispose of the tape on the right hand side.

10. Join the left hand tape to the original section of tape attached to the right hand spool. Use the same method as in procedures 6 and 7 – the only difference now is that you are joining two sections of recording tape directly together, and you are dispensing with the leader tape that was previously on the right hand side.

140

Removing unwanted speech is of course not the only reason for editing. You may also want to rearrange the running order of extracts on your rough edited tape. To do this, you again use the same general procedures described above. Begin by writing a list of the order the extracts appear on the rough edited tape, and a list of the order that you want to rearrange them into. Then splice and cut each extract in the revised order and join them end-to-end onto a 'master' spool. Always clearly mark the master spool as it is easy to mix it up with the other tapes you are cutting.

Editing cassettes is a more complicated and tricky operation because the width of the tape is so thin. Also, you have to unscrew and open up the cassette front to expose the tape reels. However, there are kits available which enable you to do this. You follow the same general principle as if you were cutting and splicing a reel to reel tape. Further instructions are usually given inside the kits. But most radio stations will insist that you use reel-to-reel tapes, because recordings made on cassette are of an inferior sound quality.

Radio workshops

If you require further assistance in making radio programmes you should contact one of the non-commercial radio/audio workshops listed in the bibliography. They are non-profit making organisations who work with interest or community groups helping them to make taped radio programmes and trying to get them broadcast on local radio stations.

Radio programmes as resource material

As well as making local radio programmes, you might also consider making use of the history features and programmes that they broadcast. Most BBC stations deposit tapes of local interest that they produce, in local libraries. They provide a valuable source of historical information, and it is sometimes possible to make arrangements to use them in exhibitions and as school resource material. The libraries which hold BBC radio tapes are listed in *The Directory of British Oral History Collections Vol. 1* (for details see bibliography).

21 Exhibitions

The importance of exhibitions

Staging an exhibition focusing upon some aspect of the life experience of local people can excite their imagination. It can lead to a deeper awareness of historical change, and a shared sense of local identity. It can give local people a sense of their own history and helps them to make sense of the past and the present.

Although in the past twenty years many museums have attempted to forge closer links with the local communities they serve, in particular, local schools, few as yet stage oral history

A local history exhibition staged by the Manchester Studies Unit.

exhibitions or use taped recollections of local people to add another dimension to their displays. There are, of course, some exceptions. For example, The Castle Museum in York uses oral history in their exhibitions, and the Passmore Edwards Museum in London lends tapes of local people's memories to schools in the area, and encourages the children to make further recordings to increase their stock. But there remains enormous scope for work in this direction.

There are two ways of going about staging an exhibition. Your group could offer to collaborate with a local museum to put on an oral history exhibition. A lot of museums would consider participating in such a project. One reason why they often don't do it by themselves, is because they are understaffed and under-financed. An offer of help could make all the difference. Or, you could organise an exhibition by yourself and stage it in local community centres, libraries, old people's homes, schools and so on. This chapter explains how to organise such an exhibition.

A theme

Every exhibition needs a theme. Without one a display loses its impact and interest, and degenerates into a hotch potch of unrelated items. Since most exhibitions will be the end product of a broader project which explores a particular period or group, your theme will be ready made for you. It might focus on schooling in the Edwardian period, The General Strike, work experience prior to the Second World War, and so on. If you are short on ideas for an organising theme, the 'School' section of the book contains lots of suggestions for projects.

Sources of exhibits

There are two main sources of exhibits. First, the documents, objects and photographs that you collect. Always give people a receipt for each item borrowed, and keep a duplicate. It should contain a fairly detailed description of each object and the information can then be used for the labels in the exhibition. On the receipt form it is often a good idea to note the condition of the object, recording any damage or imperfection when you receive it. This avoids any later argument about the damage of an item while on display.

The second source of material, is your local library, museum and record office. Their willingness to lend documents and objects often depends to a large extent upon the precautions that you are taking to ensure the safety of the exhibits. It is advisable to insure any valuable items on display, if they are not already insured by the owners.

Publicity

Good publicity is essential to attract people to your exhibition. About two weeks before it is due to begin, advertise it by displaying posters in local libraries, museums, schools, shops, and so on. You could arrange for a local press and radio feature to coincide with the opening day. If it is a large exhibition, you could invite a well known local personality to come along to open it officially. This often increases the attendance quite substantially. You might also consider arranging short talks, tape-slide shows and guided tours of the exhibitions. These are particularly useful for schoolchildren, and their provision encourages teachers to bring classes to an exhibition.

How to display items

Display your objects on strong tables and your photographs and some of your documentary material on vertical screens. If the table tops are in bad condition or are an unsuitable colour, cover them up with any woven material or kitchen paper. If someone in your group is good at do-it-yourself, he or she could easily construct screens from various wooden off cuts or soft boards. This method is cheaper as the cost of pre-constructed clip-together screens, bought new can run into several hundred pounds! You can often by-pass this problem by borrowing display equipment from the place that you have chosen to stage your exhibition. Most community centres, libraries, schools, and so on, have screens and tables which they buy specifically for display purposes.

Don't lay all your objects flat on the tables. Stand or prop some of them up to achieve a multi-dimensional effect. Also, vary

144

the size of objects displayed side by side. If you have lots of small items, try to place something large nearby, to break up the monotony.

Attractive, clear labels are an invaluable aid to the viewer of any exhibition. To ensure that they are easy to read, use Letraset for the headlines, and type the text. Although you may need to use a couple of paragraphs to introduce a theme or subject, labels should usually be short – restricted to a sentence or two of essential information. Long typewritten monographs can kill the interest of the viewer. When labelling, save words by dispensing with most adjectives. If you want to be really professional about it, there is much useful information contained in David Cordingly, *Methods of Lettering For Museums*, (available from The Museums Association, 34 Bloomsbury Way, London WC1A 2SF).

Lighting is also an important consideration in an exhibition. The lighting used in most display areas is so often dull and flat. It is not conducive to stimulating the viewer's interest and imagination. So, if possible, use spotlights to attract attention to certain objects and to add variety to the whole display. Most places where you can stage an exhibition should have spotlights that you can borrow.

Finally, it is essential that each table or vertical screen contains material which focuses upon a particular period, theme or sub-theme. A strong story line or element of continuity is necessary to hold the interest of the viewer and to make everything add up to a coherent whole. If you do not organise the material in this way, your exhibition will appear to the outsider as an accumulation of miscellaneous objects.

If you require further information, the technical aspects of staging a display are described in more detail in a straightforward manual by Atherton Harrison, *Display Staging for Amateurs*, Bell and Hyman (1969).

Tapes

Edited tapes of people's memories have enormous potential for use in association with objects or photographs displayed in exhibitions. They can create an authentic atmosphere, making the past come to life. A recorded voice, linking up with objects, photographs or perhaps a reconstructed room, gives the whole ensemble an immediate impact.

145

This impact is cheap and easy to achieve. Place the tape recorder in an appropriate position close to the relevant display item. If there is to be no constant supervision during the exhibition, it is advisable to secure the machine to something immovable to prevent theft. The tape can be operated manually by the visitors, or even better, you could use an automatically repeating loop tape. These can be bought fairly cheaply in various lengths of between one and fifteen minutes. The 'Estuary Audio' chain, which advertises in *Exchange and Mart*, sell loop tapes at the cheapest prices on the market. To make your exhibition tapes as good as possible, use the tips contained in Section 20, on how to make a radio programme. The display of photographs and tape-slide shows, both of which are important ingredients in a good exhibition, are dealt with in the following section.

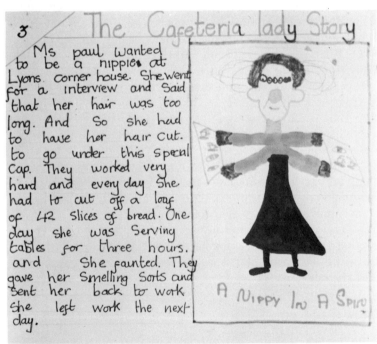

One of the exhibits from the Sweet Sixteen project.

22 Photography, tape-slide and video

There are enormous possibilities for the use of visual and audio-visual media in oral history projects. Photography, tape-slide and video are all fairly cheap and accessible media. Although the skills involved in the use of these media are straightforward and can be grasped quickly by an individual or group, it would take up too much space to describe them fully here. This section will therefore direct you to relevant articles, books and resource centres which will provide you with everything you need to know if you are planning to work in this area.

Explaining how to use a camera.

Practising in the park.

Photography

In public collections, there are often very few photographs recording the everyday life of working class communities, or even recording the life of middle and upper class people. People's family albums are of key significance in rectifying this situation. Arrange to borrow and copy interesting and important photographs contained in them.

Photographs are essential features in good local history books and exhibitions. One of the attractions of an exhibition to local people will be the opportunity to look at themselves, their

148

friends and relatives in their young days. One idea that worked at a recent East Anglian History Workshop exhibition was to place a 'comments sheet' alongside photos so that visitors could write down any details that they might remember about them – for example who was in it, and exactly when, where and why it was taken – information that we often don't know today.

If you are publishing an oral history book you will probably only be able to afford to include up to a dozen photographs in it because of reproduction costs. However, if there are good photographic collections in your locality, you might consider publishing a collection of them. For three examples of community publishers who have documented the history of their localities in this way, see *Looking Back: Photographs of Camberwell and Peckham 1860–*

The cover of A Hackney Camera 1883–1918 published by Centerprise.

1918 (Peckham Publishing Project 1977), *A Hackney Camera: Collection of Old Photographs of Hackney* (Centerprise 1974) and *A Second Look: A Photographic Record of a Walk Through Hackney in the 1800's and Today*, Centerprise (1975).

If you know nothing about photographs, one of the best introductions to the subject is Richard Greenhill, Margaret Murray and Jo Spence, *Photography* MacDonald Guidelines Series (1977). For information on copying, displaying, learning from and storing photographs see Arthur Gill, *Photographic Processes* (1980- available for £1 from The Museums Association, 34 Bloomsbury Way, London WC1A 2SF) and D. Steel and L. Taylor, *Family History in Schools*, Phillimore (1973).

For a valuable discussion of what 'community photography' is all about, and a description of the work of the main groups involved in this area, see *Camerawork No. 13: Photography in the Community* (available for 90p from Half Moon Photography Workshop, 119/121 Roman Rd, London E.2). There is an excellent article on the importance of photography in life history projects written by David Russell and the Manchester Studies Team, contained in *Camerawork No. 16* (available from the above address at the same price).

Tape-slide

Tape-slide is by far the cheapest audio-visual media you can use. The basic equipment you need is a camera, a tape recorder and a projector. Tape-slide presentations can be operated manually or automatically. Automatic playback is particularly useful in exhibitions, as it enables you to give regular, repeat performances, without having to be present yourself. It can be achieved by linking the sound track and the slides together through a synchroniser unit, which costs around £50.

In an oral history show, you can combine local voices with visuals of local people, places, documents and newspapers. The advice given in the section on how to make a radio programme will help you to put together a good soundtrack. Detailed information on the photographic and duplicating processes involved in making a tape-slide show, and suggestions on what equipment to buy, are contained in the following manuals. Martin Norgate, *Linked Tape and Slide Audio-Visual Displays* (available for 55p from The Museums Association, 34 Bloomsbury Way, London WC1A

150

2SF), *Slide-Tape For Classroom and Community* (available for £1 from The Directory For Social Change, 9 Mansfield Place, London N3) and R. Beaumont-Craggs, *Slide-Tape and Dual Projection* Focal Press (1976). Also, there is an excellent article explaining how to use tape-slide, by Caro Webb, 'Tape-Slide in Community Action, in *Camerawork No. 13* (for details see above).

Video

Video enables you to add the dimension of moving pictures to your presentation. You not only hear the voice, you also see the face of the person who is being interviewed. There is a wealth of visual detail in an interview to capture – the raised eyebrows, the gestures, the mannerisms, as well as the dress of the respondent – which complements the voice and adds interest for a potential audience.

Again, following the advice contained in the 'Radio' section of this book, should enable you to get a good sound in your oral history video production. For information on the visual side of video, how to go about buying and operating the equipment and

A video project involving young people. (From Video with Young People).

151

ideas for projects, see Tony Dowmunt, *Video With Young People*, Inter-Action Inprint (1980).

Here are a few extra tips on how to handle video on an oral history project. First, do not attempt to interview and operate the camera at the same time. It is impossible to put an interviewee at ease and maintain a natural flow of conversation if you are busy operating a camera while they are answering your questions. You need two people, one to interview and the other to film. Discuss the way in which you want to shoot the film beforehand. You need to think about questions such as, how tight should the head shots be? How should the zoom and angle shots be dealt with? How can the camera take advantage of any striking visual characteristics of the interviewee?

The interview is easier to edit if the camera operator gets a variety of shot sizes and visual angles. It can be made more interesting if the camera operator is alert to facial expressions and hand gestures. Further interest is created if you can arrange it so that your interviewee gives a demonstration, perhaps of a craft skill or an old recipe, or whatever, while he or she is talking.

During the interview the camera should be positioned facing the interviewee, shooting over the interviewer's left shoulder. After the interview it is important for the purposes of editing to shoot what are called 'reverse questions' and 'cutaways'. For reverse questions the camera should be moved to a position facing the interviewer, behind and slightly to the right of the interviewee. Then with the respondent looking at the interviewer, the interviewer should again ask the key questions that were posed during the interview. The interviewee should be asked to remain silent at this stage. These reverse questions can be inserted into the finished tape. Reverse questions help to make the final product more visually interesting. For cutaways use the same procedure but just film the interviewer listening or nodding for a few seconds. These provide useful 'joins' when you have to cut the dialogue. To add further interest you can of course shoot on location either with the interviewee or capture what they are describing, and you can use old photographs and artefacts.

152

23 Re-charging local archives

There are many local history collections throughout Britain held in libraries, museums and public records offices. They comprise artefacts, books, documents, maps, photographs and tapes relating to a particular area. You should consider cooperating with these organisations in order to ensure the long term preservation of and public access to the material you have collected, and to utilise the existing material in archives.

But very few of the artefacts of any social class in fact survive. To re-charge local archives, so that they serve local people more equally and effectively, they need inputs from and outputs into life history groups and projects.

Inputs

An oral history project should make a special effort to preserve the artefacts and records of the people whose memories it records – diaries, letters, interesting possessions, photographs, and so on. You should always ask the people whose life history you are recording whether they possess any such documents. They can be used not only as a source of historical evidence, but also for exhibitions and to illustrate books. Once they have served their immediate purpose arrangements should be made to deposit documents or artefacts in the appropriate local archive.

In some cases people may feel that certain documents are too personal to be made public, they may want copies to be taken so that they can keep the originals, or they may not want items to become public property until after their own or certain relatives deaths. In all cases their wishes must be respected. Your local archivist, curator or reference librarian will help you to make the necessary arrangements for copying and depositing.

153

You should adopt a similar principle of depositing any tape recordings and transcripts that you make in local sound archives once your project no longer has any immediate use for them. An increasing number of libraries, record offices and museums are organising facilities for storing and listening to tapes. Even if no facilities exist at present, the offer of tapes or copies may themselves stimulate the development of a small sound archive.

Outputs

Although local archives have huge gaps in their holdings, they do often contain some valuable material that can be used for display or research purposes on an oral history project. Old newspapers, political pamphlets and photographs, are three obvious examples. The local collections held by libraries and museums are listed in Adrian Brink (ed.) *The Libraries, Museums and Art Galleries Year Book 1978–79* (Cambridge 1981). Information on record offices and their holdings is contained in The Royal Commission on Historical Manuscripts, *Record Repositories in Great Britain: A Geographical Directory*, HMSO (1978).

There are over two hundred organisations in Britain which hold collections of taped life histories. Many of them provide listening facilities and public access to the tapes and some museums loan them to local schools. They are a rich source of material for life history projects. A comprehensive and detailed list of all these collections is contained in *The Directory of British Oral History Collections Vol. 1* (1981), see bibliography for details.

Bibliography

The bibliography is divided into three parts, each of which corresponds to the different sections of the book. Each section contains a guide to further reading, resources and a list of contacts and relevant organisations.

Parts one and two

Those who wish to find out more about oral history are strongly advised to read Paul Thompson's *The Voice of the Past*, Oxford University Press (1978), which contains an excellent guideline questionnaire on family life, schooling, leisure and work experience, and a comprehensive bibliography on all aspects of oral history.

Advice on buying and operating recording equipment is contained in Pete Mount and Roger Kitchen, *Tape Recording and Community Radio*, Inter-Action, (to be published 1984). For more detailed advice on interviewing and recording see Michael Winstanley, 'Some Practical Hints on Oral History Interviewing' in *Oral History* Vol. 5 no. 1 (1977). Back copies of *Oral History* are obtainable for £2.50 each from Trevor Lummis, Oral History Society, Department of Sociology, University of Essex, Wivenhoe Park, Colchester CO4 3SQ. The Oral History Society is keen to give advice and assistance to people wishing to organise oral history projects.

Many insights about presentation and interpretation can be gained by reading histories using oral sources. Those produced by commercial publishers in recent years include Ronald Blythe, *Akenfield: Portrait of An English Village* (Penguin, 1976); Mary Chamberlain, *Fenwomen* Routledge and Kegan Paul (1983); George Ewart Evans, *Ask the Fellows who Cut the Hay*, Faber (1956); *From Mouths of Men*, Faber (1976); *Where Beards Wag All: The Days that we have Seen*, Faber (1975); Angela Hewins, *The Dillen: Memories of a Man of Stratford-upon-Avon* (Elm Tree 1981); Stephen Humphries, *Hooligans or Rebels: An Oral History of Working Class Childhood and Youth 1889–1939*, Blackwell (1981); Sheila Rowbotham and Jean McCrindle, *Dutiful Daughters: Women Talk about*

155

their Lives, Allen Lane (1978); Raphael Samuel (ed.) *Village Life and Labour*, Routledge and Kegan Paul (1975); *Miners, Quarrymen and Saltworkers* Routledge and Kegan Paul (1977); *People's History and Socialist Theory* Routledge and Kegan Paul (1980); Studs Terkel, *Working*, Wildwood House (New York 1974); Paul Thompson, *The Edwardians*, Weidenfeld and Nicolson (1975); Thea Thompson, *Edwardian Childhoods*, Routledge and Kegan Paul (1980); Jerry White, *Rothschild Buildings: Life in an East End Tenement 1887–1920*, Routledge and Kegan Paul (1980). Oral history books produced by community publishers are listed on page 162.

Part three

One of the best beginner's guides to family history which contains an extensive bibliography on all aspects of family history is Don Steel, *Discovering Your Family History*, BBC Publications (1980). Essential reading for anyone beginning a project with schoolchildren is D. Steel and L. Taylor, *Family History in Schools*, Phillimore Books (1973). Also useful are P. Grafton, *You, You and You: The People out of Step with World War 2*, Pluto (1981), M. Mander, *How to Trace Your Ancestors*, Mayflower Books (1977), and J. Dixon and D. Flack, *Preserving Your Past: A Painless Guide to Writing Your Autobiography and Family History*, Doubleday (New York 1977). Journals with articles and information on family history are as follows: *Family History News and Digest*; *Family History, The Journal of Heraldic and Genealogical Studies*; *Genealogists Magazine*; and *The Local Historian*. A list of names and addresses of Family History Societies appears in D. Steel (see above).

A useful introduction for teachers wishing to use oral history methods and materials in schools is Sallie Purkis, *Oral History in Schools*, published by the Oral History Society for 75p + 25p postage. The Manchester Studies Unit of Manchester Polytechnic have produced a history pack, *Hurrah For A Life in the Factory* which uses oral history and which is available on loan to schools. For examples of the use of life history in schools to counter racial prejudice and to develop the confidence of young people from other countries, see Chris Searle, *The World in a Classroom*, Writers and Readers Cooperative (1977) and *Our Lives*, available from ILEA English Centre, Sutherland St, London SW1, for £1.75p. Eliot Wigginton's Foxfire Project in America is described in *The Foxfire Book*, Doubleday/Anchor (1972), *Foxfire One-Three*, Doubleday/Anchor (1975) and *Foxfire Five*, Doubleday/Anchor (1979). Oral history resource material for schools has been produced in two BBC Schools Radio series *People Talking* (enquiries to Janet Whitaker, BBC Schools Radio, Broadcasting House, London

156

W1A 1AA), and in the series *From Scotland's Past* (enquiries to Marinell Ash, BBC, 5 Queen St, Edinburgh EH2 1JF).

Many ideas for the use of life history in literacy projects are contained in Jane Mace, *Working with Words: Literacy Beyond School*, Writers and Readers Cooperative (1979) and in the journal *Write First Time* (enquiries to Westbourne Road Centre, Bedford MK40 1JD), which gives a voice to adult literacy students. A collection of the writings of adult literacy students is contained in *Writing*, Federation of Worker Writers and Community Publishers (1978). For a discussion of the significance of the FWWCP and examples of its work see *The Republic of Letters: Working Class Writing and Local Publishing*, Comedia (1982).

Help The Aged have produced three Reminiscence Aid slide-tape packs for use with the elderly called *Recall*. Part 1, *Childhood: The Great War*, Part 2 *Youth and Adult Life; Living Through the 30's*, and Part 3, *The Second World War: A Different World*. Each pack contains 40 slides and a cassette, and they cost £12 each. A recall handbook explaining how to use the material is available for £3. For details contact Help the Aged Education Department, 318 St Paul's Road, London N1. There are now many reminiscence aid projects and reminiscence socials taking place. For details of what is happening in your area contact Help the Aged (see above) or Age Concern (Head Office: Bernard Sunley House, 60 Pitcairn Road, Mitcham, London SW17).

A taste of what oral history is all about is provided for junior school children in the series 'Into the Past' published by Longmans. The books have been compiled from information collected by children talking to old people they know. Titles in the series so far are Sallie Purkis *At Home in 1900*; *In the Street in 1900*; *At School in 1900*; and Elizabeth Merson *In the Country in 1900*. Another oral history book which is compiled from material collected by pupils in junior schools is *Arbury is Where We Live* (available from EARO, Back Hill, Ely, Cambridgeshire).

For work produced by older people see the publications of the East Bowling History Workshop, *Bowling Tidings* (1979), *East Bowling Reflections* (1980) and *Gateway to Education* (1981).

An excellent booklet by Ruth Richardson, *Making History: The Factory* shows you how to write a history of the factory where you work or once worked, or any factory that you are interested in. It is available free from TV History Workshop, 42 Queen's Square, London WC1N 3AJ.

A list of the names and addresses of local history societies appears in *Local History Societies in England and Wales: A List* (1978) – available from The Standing Conference for Local History, 26 Bedford Square, London WC1B 3HU. The Standing Conference also produces a quarterly journal *The Local Historian*.

Some recent local history titles which have a strong oral history element are as follows:

Batheaston Remembers: Village life 1883–1940. Available from The Batheaston Society, Eagle Cottage, 110 Northend, Batheaston, Nr. Bath. Edith Hall *Canary Girls and Stockpots*. The 'Canary Girls' of the title were girls in the munition factories whose 'skins were yellow through working with explosive chemicals'. Available from Luton WEA Barnfield College, New Bedford Road, Luton, Beds. Winifred Nicol *Growing Up in Gloucester*. Available from Centre for the Study of Rural Society, Bishop Grosseteste College, Lincoln LN1 3DY. *Memories of Saltley: No. 1 The Railwaymen*. Available from Saltley WEA, Saltley Action Centre, 2 Alum Rock Rd, Birmingham 8. Maggie Newbury *Reminiscences of a Bradford Mill Girl*. Available from Local Studies Advisor, Bradford Central Library, Bradford. Sylvia Bond (Ed) *Yesteryears: School, Work and Leisure*. Available from Sylvia Bond, 31 Holmesdale Road, Highgate, London N6. Elizabeth Roberts, *Working Class Barton and Lancaster 1890–1930*. Available from Centre for North East Regional Studies, University of Lancaster. Dave Russell and George Walker, *Trafford Park 1896–1939*. Available from Manchester Studies, Manchester Polytechnic, Hilton House, Hilton St, Manchester M1 2FE. Billy Kay (ed), *Odyssey: Voices from Scotland's Recent Past*, Nos 1 and 2. Compilations from BBC Scotland's Odyssey series. Available from Polygon Books, 1 Buccleuch Place, Edinburgh EH8 9LW, price £5.95 each.

A *History Workshop Journal* is produced twice yearly. Details about subscriptions and back numbers can be obtained from the Business Manager, History Workshop, PO Box 69, Oxford OX2 7XA.

The Oral History Society produces a twice yearly journal, *Oral History*. Information on how to join the Society and subscribe to the journal can be obtained from Trevor Lummis, Oral History Society, Department of Sociology, University of Essex, Wivenhoe Park, Colchester CO4 3SQ.

List of local groups using oral history
All of the following involve socialist or feminist historians:
Arbroath History Project, Graham Smith, Hospitalfield House, Arbroath, Sutherland.
Birmingham Feminist History Group, Catherine Hall, 65 Prospect Rd, Mosley, Birmingham 13.
Bolton Oral History Project, Central Library, Le Mans Crescent, Bolton, BL1 1SA.
Bradford History Workshop, Tony Jowitt, Adult Education Centre, Mornington Villas, Bradford 8.
Communist Party History Group, Geoff Ferres, 19 Rodgers St, Summertown, Oxford.
Dublin History Workshop, Tom Weldon, 82a Ballygall Rd, W. Finglas,

Dublin 11, Eire; and Sean Hutton 16 Cambridge Ave., Bridlington, E. Yorks.

Ealing Oral History Group, Hanwell Community Centre, Westcott Crescent, London W7.

East Anglian History Workshop, Brenda Corti, Department of Sociology, University of Essex, Colchester.

East Bowling History Workshop, 75 Brompton Rd, Bradford BD4 7JE.

Edinburgh History Workshop, Bill Knox, 4 South Elgin St, Edinburgh EH7 5NH.

Feminist History Group (London) Anna Davin, 73 Balfour St, London SE17.

Grimsby Oral History Group, Peter Gould, 90 Legsby Ave, Grimsby, S. Humberside DN32 ONE.

Holberry Society for the Study of Sheffield Labour History, Sam Holmes, 74 Emerson Cresc., Sheffield 5.

Huddersfield History Workshop, Cyril Pearce, Bretton Hall College of Higher Education, West Bretton, Wakefield, W. Yorks WF4 4LG.

Hull History Workshop, Dave Marson, 81 Compass Rd, Beverley, Hull.

Irish Labour History Society, Francis Devine, c/o ICTU, 1 Grand Parade, Dublin 16.

Isle of Dogs Project, Bernard Canavan and Eve Hostettler, 151 Manchester Rd, London E4.

Kent History Workshop. David Ormrod, Eliot College, The University, Canterbury.

Lambeth and Southwark History Workshop, Dave Russell, 53 Fernleigh House, Vestry Rd, London SE6

London History Workshop Centre, 42 Queen's Square, Holborn, London WC1.

London Women's History Group, c/o Women's Research and Resource Centre, 190 Upper Street, London N1.

North East Group of the Society for the Study of Labour History, Joan Knott, 79 Woodburn Square, Whitley Bay, Tyne and Wear.

North Staffordshire Labour Studies Groups, Malcolm Spiers, c/o North Staffs Poly, College Rd, Stoke-on-Trent ST4 2DE.

North West Communist Party History Group, Margaret Cohen, 6 Higher Downs, Altrincham, Cheshire.

Paisley People's History Project, Sean Damet, Department of Social Studies, Paisley College of Technology, High St, Paisley, PA1 2BE.

People's history of the Dulais Valley, Hywel Francis, South Wales Miner's Library, 50 Sketty Rd, Swansea SA2 OLG.

People's History Project, Morley College, Westminster Bridge Rd, London SE1.

Scotland Road Local History Group, 6 Tatlock Tower, Tatlock St, Liverpool L5 8XA.

Scottish Communist Party History Group, John Foster, 9 Tarausay St, Glasgow 15.

Scottish Labour History Society, Ian MacDougall, 4 East Preston St, Edinburgh EH8 9QA.

Scottish Oral History Group, Ian Flett, Dundee Archivist, City Square, Dundee.

Sheffield and South Yorkshire History Workshop, John Baster, Economic History Dept, The University, Sheffield.

Shetland Community History Project, Brian Smith, Shetland Archives, Brentham House, 5 Harbour St, Lerwick, Shetland.

Sussex Society for the Study of Labour History, Alun Hawkins, Arts B, University of Sussex, Falmer, Brighton.

Television History Workshop, 42 Queen's Sq, Holborn, London WC1.

Tower Hamlets Arts Project, 178 Whitechapel Rd, London E1.

Ulster Society for Oral History, Clive Cochrane, The Queen's University of Belfast, Belfast BT7 1NN, N. Ireland.

West Midlands Group for the Study of Labour History, John Benson, Dept of Arts, The Polytechnic, Wudfana St, Wolverhampton.

West Midlands Oral History Group, Pam Taylor, c/o Winterbourne, Edgbaston Park Rd, Birmingham 15.

Yorkshire, Humberside and North Midlands Group of the Society for the Study of Labour History, Geoff Brown, Sutton Centre, High Pavement, Sutton-in-Ashfield, Notts.

How to start a new group

If there is no group meeting near you, or where you live, why not start one up? Every Adult Education Institute runs day and evening classes. If you would like them to run a group on local history contact the Warden or the Community Education Worker who will be happy to discuss your ideas. Similarly the Worker's Education Association, Central Office, 32 Tavistock Square, London WC1 (01-387-8966), runs many classes and may be able to help you set up a group in your area. Another approach is to contact your local community centre and ask them about setting up an oral history group.

The Federation of Worker Writers and Community Publishers is open to all groups engaged in the promotion or practice of working class writing and community publishing. To qualify for membership, groups should have published work in some form, or be in the process of doing so.

Federation of Worker Writers & Community Publishers

(for more information about the FWWCP write to 6 Twiss St, Liverpool 8)

160

List of member groups:

Basement Writers,
  Old Town Hall,
  Cable St, London E1
Bristol Broadsides,
  110 Cheltenham Rd,
  Bristol BS6 5RW
  (0272 40491)
Centerprise Publishing Project,
  136 Kingsland High St,
  London E8
  (01 254 9632/5)
Commonplace Workshop,
  28 Dorset Rd,
  Ealing, London W5
Commonword Writers'
  Workshop,
  61 Bloom St,
  Manchester M1 3LY
  (061 236 2773)
East Bowling History
  Workshop,
  c/o Secretary,
  75 Brompton Rd.,
  Bradford BD4 7JE
  (0274 391268)
Gatehouse Project,
  St Luke's, Sawley Rd,
  Miles Platting,
  Manchester 10
  (061 205 9522)
Hackney Writers' Workshop,
  c/o Centerprise
Liverpool 8 Writers' Workshop,
  6 Twiss St, Liverpool 8
  (051 728 8301)
London Voices,
 70 Holden Rd,
  London N12
  (01 346 5291)
Netherley & District
  Writers' Workshop,
  38 Glebe Hey,
  Netherley, Liverpool 27
  (051 498 4735)

Old Swan Writers' Workshop,
  c/o 30 Fieldway,
  Liverpool 15
Peckham Publishing Project,
  The Bookplace,
  13 Peckham High St,
  London SE15
  (01 701 1757)
Peckham Writers,
  (address as above)
People's Publications,
  34 Fenham Rd,
  Newcastle upon Tyne
  NE4 5PB
  (09632 761351)
Queen Spark Books,
  13 West Drive,
  Brighton (0273 682855)
Scotland Road Writers'
  Workshop
  123 Logan Towers, Athol St,
  Liverpool 5 (051 207 6518)
SE1 People's History Group,
  c/o 10 Brief St,
  London SE5 (01 852 4700)
Stepney Books,
  19 Tomlins Grove,
  London E3 (01 790 6420)
Tollcross Writer's Workshop,
  Riddle's Court,
  322 Lawnmarket,
  Edinburgh EH1 2PG
  (031 226 3456)
Tottenham Writers' Workshop,
  Drayton Community Centre,
  Gladesmore Rd.,
  London N15
Tower Hamlets Worker
  Writers,
  178 Whitechapel Rd,
  London E1
  (01 247 0216)
Voices,
  61 Bloom St,

Manchester M1 3LY
(061 236 2773)
Women and Words,
137 Newton Rd,
Sparkhill, Birmingham
(021 733 6063)

Word and Action Publications,
23 Beaucroft Lane,
Wimbourne, Dorset
Write First Time,
Westbourne Road Centre,
Bedford MK40 1JD
(0234 64454)

A select list of books produced by the Federation of Worker Writers and Community Publishers

All are individual or group autobiographies except where otherwise stated.

Ron Barnes *A Licence to Live* (1974) and *Coronation Cups and Jam Jars* (1976), Centerprise

H. J. Bennett *I was a Walworth Boy*, Peckham Publishing Project (1980)

Ernie Benson *To Struggle is to Live – 2 Vols*, People's Publications (1980)

John Boler and Ken Worpole *Hackney Half Term Adventure* – a school reading book, Centerprise (1972)

Bowling Tidings, East Bowling History Workshop (1979)

Bristol as We Remember It, Bristol Broadsides (1980)

Bristol's Radical History, Bristol Broadsides (1983)

Joyce Crump *The Ups and Downs of Being Born*, Vassall Neighbourhood Council (1980)

Dolly David *A Sense of Adventure*, SE1 People's History Group (1980)

The Island: The Life and Death of an East End London Community – 1870–1970, Centerprise (1979)

A. S. Jaspar *A Hoxton Childhood*, Centerprise (1973)

Martha Lang *The Austrian Cockney*, Centerprise (1980)

Leslie Mildiner & Bill House *The Gates*, Stepney Basement Writers and Centerprise (1975)

Les Moss *Live and Learn: A Life and Struggle for Progress*, Queen Spark (1979)

Daisy Noakes *The Town Beehive: A Young Girl's Lot, Brighton 1910–1934* (1980) and *Faded Rainbow: Our Married Life*, Queen Spark (1980)

Florrie Roberts *The Ups and Downs of Florrie Roberts*, Peckham Publishing Project

Shush Mum's Writing (1978) and *Shush Mum's Writing Again* – working class women's poetry, Bristol Broadsides (1981)

Stepney Words – poetry by comprehensive schoolchildren, Centerprise (1973)

Tough Annie from Suffragette to Stepney Councillor, Stepney Books (1980)

Toby: A Bristol Tramp Tells His Story, Bristol Broadsides (1980)

Voices A regular magazine containing articles, stories, poems and information from members of the federation (Federation of Worker Writer's and Community Publishers)

Jim Wolveridge *Ain't it Grand: This was Stepney*, Stepney Books (1976)

Ken Worpole *Local Publishing and Local Culture* – an account of the Centerprise publishing project 1972–1977, Centerprise (1977)

Working Lives Vol. 1 Twelve Accounts of Work 1905–1945 (1976) and *Working Lives Vol. 2 1945–1977*, Centerprise (1977)

Writing descriptions of the groups in the FWWCP and selections from the work they have published, Federation of Worker Writers and Community Publishers (1978)

Part four

For advice on publishing and marketing your material see Jonathan Zeitlyn, *Print: How You Can Do It Yourself* (Inter-Action 1980); Keith Smith, *Marketing for Small Publishers* (Inter-Action 1980) and Denis MacShane, *Using the Media*, Pluto (1979). Practical information about contacts and outlets can be found in *Willings Press Guide* (East Grinstead – updated each year) and The Writers and Artists Yearbook (Adam and Charles Black – updated each year). For fund raising see *The Directory of Grant Making Trusts 1981*, Charities Aid Foundation Publications Ltd (1981) and Andrew Phillips and Keith Smith, *Charitable Status: A Practical Handbook*, Inter-Action (1980).

Information on exhibitions, photography, tape-slide and video are contained in Atherton Harrison, *Display Staging For Amateurs*, Bell (1969); Richard Greenhill, Margaret Murray and Jo Spence, *Photography*, McDonald Guidelines Series (1977); Arthur Gill, *Photographic Processes* (1980 – available for £1 from the Museums Association, 34 Bloomsbury Way, London WC1A 2SF); D. Steel and L. Taylor, *Family History in Schools* op. cit.; *Camerawork No. 13* and *No. 16*, available for 90p each from Half Moon Photography Workshop 119/121 Roman Rd, London E2; Martin Nortgate, *Linked Tape and Slide Audio-Visual Displays*, available for 55p from Museums Association – address above; *Slide Tape for Classroom and Community*, available for £1 from The Directory For Social Change, 9 Mansfield Place, London N3; R. Beaumont-Craggs, *Slide-Tape and Dual Projection* (Focal Press 1976); and Tony Dowmunt, *Video with Young People*, Inter-Action (1981). For collections of old photographs rescued by community groups see *Looking Back: Photographs of Camberwell and Peckham 1860–1918*, Peckham Publishing Project (1977); *A Hackney Camera: Collection of Old Photographs of Hackney*, Centerprise (1974); *A Second Look: A Photographic Record of a Walk Through Hackney in the 1890s and Today*, Centerprise (1975); and *Family Albums 1880–1950: Photographs From the Family Albums of Working People*, Manchester Studies (1982).

List of non-commercial radio/audio workshops

1. Local Radio Workshop,
   12 Praed Mews,
   London W2
   (01-402 7651).
   Contact: Gloria George
   or Thomas O'Mally.
   Women's Airwaves, Black
   Women's Radio Group and
   Best of the News can all
   be contacted through
   Local Radio Workshop.

2. Audio Workshop,
   Inter-Action,
   15 Wilkin Street,
   London NW5 3NG
   (01-267 9421).
   Contact: Pete Mount
   or Tim Carruthers

3. Islington Local
   Radio Group,
   Islington Bus Company,
   Palmers Place,
   London N7
   (01-609 0226).
   Contact: Carlos Ordonez

4. Radio Doom,
   31–33 Derby Road,
   Southport,
   Merseyside PR8 1JP
   (0704 42149/60118).

5. Commonsound Radio
   Resource,
   c/o 39 Everton Road,
   Sheffield 10

   (0742 686369).
   Contact: Chris Mead

6. Yorkshire Arts Association
   Communications Centre,
   21 Chapel Street,
   Bradford 1
   (0274 722769)
   Contact: Alf Bower

7. Hill College of
   Further Education
   Sound Studio Workshop,
   Inglemire Avenue,
   Hull HU6 7LU
   (0482 42157).

8. Greater Manchester
   Radio Action,
   St Thomas Centre,
   Ardwick Green North,
   Manchester M12 6FZ
   (061 273 7451).
   Contact: Dawn Moseley,
   Bernadette Jeffers

9. Walworth Cable Radio,
   Shop 8, Taplow,
   Aylesbury Estate,
   London SE18
   (01-701 9010).
   Contact: Caroline Mitchell

10. Northants Radio Project,
    14a Wantage Road,
    Abingdon, Northampton
    (0604-408-978).
    Contact: Roger Fitzhugh

For a discussion of the importance of local archives see Bill Williams and Audrey Linkman, *Recovering the People's Past: The Archive Rescue Programme of Manchester Studies* in *History Workshop Journal no. 8* (Autumn 1979). All the British oral history collections in universities, museums, libraries, record offices, and so on, which at present numbers around 230, are listed in detail and indexed in *The Directory of British Oral History Collections Vol. 1* available for £1.95 + 25p postage from

Trevor Lummis, Oral History Society, Department of Sociology, University of Essex, Wivenhoe Park, Colchester CO4 3SQ.

John Richardson *The Local Historian's Encyclopaedia* (London 1982). A useful guide to the documentary materials you can use for local history research. Available from Historical Publications, Orchard House, Station Rd, New Barnet, Herts. £4.50 including postage.

Ruth Richardson's *Making History – The Factory*, shows you how to write a history of the factory where you work or once worked. It is available, free, from 42 Queen Square, London WC1N 3AJ.

Finally, *The Making of Modern London 1815–1914*, Sidgwick & Jackson (1983), written by Gavin Weightman and myself to accompany the TV series should be a useful starting point for those studying London's history.

Inter-Action

Inter-Action is the umbrella name for Inter-Action Trust Limited and its ten associated charitable companies and trusts. Founded in 1968 by Ed Berman to stimulate community involvement and to experiment with uses of creativity, it is based in a purpose-built centre in the London Borough of Camden.

The twenty working teams within Inter-Action cover a wide range of activities, some of which are: a community media service, a soft adventure playroom, City Farm 1, a community print-shop and the Sports-Space Project for increasing the usage of inner city sports areas.

Inter-Action's educational activities include an alternative education project for truants, a compensatory arts programme named the Weekend Arts College, an unusual farmyard-on-wheels known as the Animobile and Make-It-Yourself which is a new community education programme to guide young people through a learn-as-you-do-it project to design, manufacture and market their own product.

Amongst Inter-Action's theatre projects are a children's and community theatre troupe known as Dogg's Troupe, the British American Repertory Company and the Captain Cook and William Shakespeare Cameos.

Much of Inter-Action's experience is made available to other voluntary groups through the Advisory Service and Training Unit which includes an architectural service. A range of training courses are available for those interested in community action, community arts and the uses of drama. These are backed-up by workshops and seminars on organisational and management matters as they concern the voluntary sector. Inprint, the publishing unit, issue practical guides on topics of interest to voluntary and community groups, playscripts and training materials on co-operative employment.

Further information is available from Inter-Action, 15 Wilkin Street, London NW5 3NG, 01-267 9421.